We at Trafford believe that it is the responsibility of us all, as both individuals and corporations, to make choices that are environmentally and socially sound. You, in turn, are supporting this responsible conduct each time you purchase a Trafford book, or make use of our publishing services. To find out how you are helping, please visit www.trafford.com/responsiblepublishing.html

Our mission is to efficiently provide the world's finest, most comprehensive book publishing service, enabling every author to experience success. To find out how to publish your book, your way, and have it available worldwide, visit us online at www.trafford.com/10510

Trafford
PUBLISHING®

www.trafford.com

North America & international
toll-free: 1 888 232 4444 (USA & Canada)
phone: 250 383 6864 • fax: 250 383 6804
email: info@trafford.com

The United Kingdom & Europe
phone: +44 (0)1865 722 113 • local rate: 0845 230 9601
facsimile: +44 (0)1865 722 868 • email: info.uk@trafford.com

10 9 8 7 6 5 4 3 2 1

WORDS OF PRAISE FOR

Holy Change: A Systemic Approach to Transforming a Community

In his book, *Holy Change: A Systemic Approach to Transforming a Community*, Joseph Parker blends together solid Biblical principles with uncommon common sense as he calls the church of Jesus Christ to be committed to both the spiritual transformation of persons and the social transformation of places. With the insight of one who has "been there and done that" he says, "I now see neighborhood transformation as kingdom building rather than the social engagement of the church with a neighborhood." After reading this book so do I.

If you are interested in the whole gospel for the whole world by the whole church you should take hold of this book and let it take hold of you.

Paul W. Powell
Former Dean, George W. Truett Theological Seminary
Baylor University

****

"At the dawn of the 21st century the global city continues to challenge both civic and religious leaders to respond to its complex and ever changing contours...new immigrants, old and new poverty, and simplistic and old solutions. *Holy Change* by Dr. Joseph C. Parker, Jr. offers us a sound biblical-theological approach to community transformation that should be noted by all change agents - inside or outside the church."

Dr. Eldin Villafañe,
Professor of Christian Social Ethics,
Gordon-Conwell Theological Seminary

Rev. Joseph C. Parker, Jr.

TABLE OF CONTENTS

ACKNOWLEDGEMENTS

This book is dedicated to my wife of 31 years, J. LaVerne, who loves and believes in me enough to encourage and prod me for some time to write this book. She is the "Georgia wind" beneath my wings. I also dedicate it to my three daughters – Jessica LaVerne, Jennifer LaVonne and Janetta LaVelle – whose sweet love continues to stir in me the desire to transform communities in which they can live and find peace.

I also dedicate this book to my late father, "Morehouse brother," pastor, and father-in-the ministry, Rev. Dr. Joseph C. Parker, Sr. and mother Addie Ruth Fox Parker for depositing in me through their lives an understanding of Christian faith and love for ministry and a commitment that the church should be concerned about the community and whole person. I am so blessed and proud that they were part of the founding of the Montgomery (Alabama) Improvement Association and Alabama Civil Rights Movement, a wonderful example of how the Black church led to the transformation of communities.

May my sisters – Marvice, Gail, Lynne, and Linda – who are all women of faith, know their lifelong love and encouragement have shaped, clothed and sustained me.

May this book also be dedicated to my father-in-the-ministry and pastoral predecessor, the late Rev. James E. Obey, Sr., who truly nurtured me as his son, helped me process my call to ministry, taught me about ministry and gave me opportunities to practice it, and prepared me to succeed him as David Chapel's pastor and a community transformer.

May this book also be dedicated to my other family pastors who have encouraged and supported me immeasurably throughout my ministry, my father-by-marriage, retired Pastor O. L. Morris (Macon, Georgia) and my brother-by-marriage, Pastor Todd M. Wheelock (New Vision Church, Houston, Texas).

May this book also be dedicated to the David Chapel Missionary Baptist Church, the congregation I have been allowed to pastor for more than 15 years and whose love continues to stir and drive me on; the congregation that I came to as a member in which I answered God's call, developed and practiced my ministry and was chosen to lead in 1992 into the 21st Century; the congregation that has allowed me to learn through them how a congregation can participate in transforming a community. I also dedicate this book to the wonderful people in the Chestnut neighborhood in Austin, Texas that I have grown to love.

May this book also be dedicated to my other father-in-the-ministry, the late Dr. E. K. Bailey and the Concord Missionary Baptist Church of Dallas, Texas, of which my wife and I were members from 1976-79. It was there that I experienced a wonderful pastor-people relationship that helped soften my heart for my call to ministry and the pastorate. Dr. Bailey spiritually nurtured me as I ran from my call to ministry, advised me in my ministry, installed me as a pastor, modeled and demonstrated how to lead the local church to be more relevant to one's generation.

I further dedicate this book to my alma mater, Morehouse College, the peerless institution for men that nurtured and educated me in so many ways and my past and present "Morehouse brothers," including my father, who have established and are establishing the Morehouse tradition of being community transformers. They continue to challenge me to reach the crown that is placed above my head, daring me – and all Morehouse Men – to grow tall enough to wear it. I also dedicate this to "my sons" and Morehouse brothers, Jeremy D. Battle, my son-by-marriage and Rev. Kevin Rae Miles Johnson, the pastor of the Bright Hope Baptist Church in Philadelphia, whom I starting mentoring when he was in middle school, both of whom are community transformers in the making.

I also thank my pastoral covenant-brothers of more than ten years – Pastors Larry Bethune, Ashton Cumberbatch, Jr., Ralph Daniels, Geno Hildebrandt, Elijah Holland, Rick Randall, and Elvin Tyrone – for their love, prayers, support, and exhortation. In the midst of our efforts to be community transformers in our city we continue to teach each other that "a friend loves at all times and a brother is born for adversity" (Proverbs 17:17).

Finally, I dedicate this book to the George W. Truett Theological Seminary of Baylor University that sharpened my theological and analytical understanding and preparation for ministry. May this book also be dedicated to my doctoral professors, Dr. Eldin Villafañe, Douglas and Judy Hall of the Gordon-Conwell Theological Seminary Boston campus who taught me about urban ministry from a systemic perspective, which led to my thinking written in this book.

I am also grateful to my editor, Greg Bailey, for his helpful insights and advice in reviewing my manuscript and Pamela Marvels, my Executive Assistant, and Jolene Hall, my former Executive Assistant, for their assistance. Thanks is also given to Evelyn Alemanni for her layout and cover design.

To God be the glory!

Austin, Texas

FOREWORD

*J*esus loved the city. He loved the city so much until he died for the city outside of the gates of the city. Yet there is a modern tendency for churches to abandon the city. Many churches seek mega-church status and in order to accomplish this goal they move into upward mobility suburbia where they can preach a nice, neat, well manicured suburban gospel, without remembering to share their resources with the poor, powerless, and voiceless marginalized of the city. But Doctor Joseph Parker not only calls the church to love the city with the compassion of Jesus, he challenges the church to actualize a systemic approach for transformation of the city. His approach is grounded in his success in Austin, Texas where he applied the hexagon technique in the Chestnut neighborhood. I have visited this community and I am impressed with the success of the approaches used in transforming the Chestnut neighborhood.

Students of urban ministry will be helped in developing a theology of urban ministry that includes a theology of place, peace, and prayer. Insights can be studied in depth as readers study the expansive bibliography of urban scholars like Raymond J. Bakke and Eldin Villafañe. I commend *Holy Change: A Systemic Approach to Transforming A Community* to you. May this work inspire us to move beyond introversion to extroversion to be God's Shalom to the dirt poor in the slums and hovels in the cities of the two thirds world where half of the world's citizens live on less than subsistence wages of $2.00 a day, a world where water is polluted and medical care is unknown and malnutrition is wide spread.

Dr. J. Alfred Smith, Sr.
Senior Pastor, Allen Temple Baptist Church, Oakland, California
and Professor of Christian Ministry and Preaching,
American Baptist Seminary of the West, Berkeley, California

INTRODUCTION

Not long ago, I was riding in my car in the city in which I live, preach, and pastor. I had just heard some news reports and read the local morning newspaper, and I started thinking about some of the issues my community faced. It seemed that wherever I turned, I heard or read about moral and ethical quagmires; a feeling of lostness; conflict and strained relations between neighbors; strained relations between citizens and community institutions; racial and cultural tensions; broken marriages and families; allegations of unjust social, educational, economic and political systems; destruction of life; and overall quality-of-life concerns. It seemed clear to me that things in my city needed to change.

But these are not new issues. They have been perpetual issues in my community. And these ongoing challenges are not unique to my city. Many of these issues have confronted American communities for a long time, and my guess is that reading newspapers from twenty-five or more years ago would reveal that many of these pressing issues existed even then.

So what is going on here? Perhaps it has something to do with the nature of cities. Indeed, there are those who believe "[t]he city is the locus of a great and continuing battle between the God of Israel and/or the church and the god of the world."[1] Numerous examples from the past reveal how righteousness and unrighteousness have long co-existed in cities:

- Jerusalem and the other cities of ancient Judah[2] were places of ongoing and active spiritual warfare against evil, and that warfare caused problems that beckoned for transformation. Jerusalem had the presence of God and was a gathering place for nations[3], but it was also a place of violence and rebellion.

- Sodom and Gomorrah had a remnant of righteous inhabitants who had a relationship with God and were concerned about the welfare of others[4]. But there were also wicked inhabitants who were full of pride, idolatry, and selfishness.

- Nineveh was a great and wealthy city[5]. But it was also wicked, full of lies, oppression, and exploitation.

- Babylon was a city of power and abundant resources[6]. But it was also a place of idolatry and corruption.

- The New Testament city of Corinth was a prosperous commercial and military center, and many Christians lived there. But it also was an immoral and wicked city, with one thousand "sacred prostitutes" at its temple of Aphrodite[7].

- Ephesus was a religious, commercial, and political center, and another city with a large Christian population. But it also was a place of idolatry, as seen in the temple worship of Sarapis, the Egyptian deity, and Artemis, the fertility goddess that was considered one of the seven wonders of the ancient world[8].

The positive and negative attributes found in the biblical cities and their inhabitants also can be found in the cities and suburbs of today. We can see the relationship between the sin of the city and the sin of the people. Our cities serve as the battleground for the struggle between righteousness and evil. Therefore, we must acknowledge the existence of "personal and social sin and evil" in our cities[9]. And we must see that this problem is due to the nature of our cities.

Meredith Kline informs our understanding of "the city." He considers Genesis 4:1–6:8 and observes:

There we have the record both of an original, normal order when the city of God was mandated in the stipulations of the creational covenant and of the subsequent common grace order and its provision of the city, not now the city of God but the city in a form adapted to the abnormal situation following upon the Fall. [10]

Kline believes that Genesis 4:15, God's promise of the preservation of Cain, is a virtual city charter, as seen in Lamech's boasts about his reign in Genesis 4:24. Consequently, God authorized the post-fall city through a divine pronouncement to Cain, ordaining an order of law and creating a political structure, through common grace, in the wilderness.[11] Soon afterward, a "city"[12] came into existence. Therefore, the city was mandated as an interim refuge from the wilderness after Adam and Eve's banishment from paradise.[13] It was and is a temporary place that was given for the benefit of humankind by an act of God's grace and mercy.

Without doubt, the city of today is a place where sin and evil dwell and seek dominance. Its human dwellers are self-centered and full of carnality. It is a place where people have forsaken God's rule and followed the stubbornness of their hearts. It is a place of idolatry, oppression, violence, and exploitation. The city is a place that calls for God's judgment.[14]

But the city also is a place of good and righteous living. It is a place of human achievement.[15] It is a place where bumper stickers on cars encourage people to practice intentional and random acts of kindness. It is a place where the hungry are fed, homeless people find shelter, abandoned children are adopted, and the poor are clothed. It is a place inhabited by those who are created in the image of God but scarred by sin. It is to be a place where health, harmony, justice, prosperity, and welfare reside personally, socially, and systemically, being accessible to all the inhabitants. Some observers might conclude that the city almost has a split personality, resulting from sin's corruption. Nevertheless, God loves the city[16] and desires for it to be a place where all can live peaceably.

Of course, the easy, short-cut answer for why problems exist and our cities require transformation is sin. But I believe there are other considerations that will not allow us to glibly attribute our problems only to sin.

I live in a city that is almost 170 years old, where the good news of Jesus Christ has been "witnessed" for almost as long[17] and where thousands, if not millions, of Christians have lived and practiced their faith, and where churches have existed. So I wondered why my city was continuing to experience these nagging, divisive, and disruptive issues, beckoning for transformation. Indeed, I wondered the same thing about the historical racist environment of my hometown of Birmingham, Alabama, during the 1950s and 1960s. I wondered why other cities that were occupied by Christians and churches were in the same situation. Why had the witnessing of the good news of Jesus Christ not caused our cities to change?

Since city problems are fundamentally people problems, and since God has chosen to work through people, perhaps the challenge has to do with the difficulties involved in bringing about real change in the behavior of people, in and the systems and institutions they operate. One writer has said, "People change what they do less because they are given *analysis* that shifts their *thinking* than because they are *shown* a truth that influences their *feelings*,"[18] or one could say, their hearts. An unknown person said, "Until the pain of remaining the same hurts more than the pain of change, people prefer to remain the same." Yet, the Bible says, "Be transformed by the renewing of your mind."[19] Which is it? Can we change people through influencing their feelings, touching their hearts, or renewing their minds? Perhaps it is all of these, so long as "truth" is involved. In any event, could it not be that "changed" people transform communities?

My prayer is that my city and all cities will become transformed and revitalized places of peace that will live out God's intentions. Accordingly, this book addresses four (4) needs:

1. The need for churches to be committed to and involved in community development and community transformation.

2. The need to understand the system or social reality related to transforming or revitalizing a community.

3. The need to consider one example of how a community – the Chestnut neighborhood in Austin, Texas – has approached community transformation relative to land use and transportation, environment and parks, housing, economic development, public safety, youth, and health issues.

4. The need for churches to have an effective model for partnering with a community, government, and businesses for the purpose of community development and community transformation.

This book also considers the challenges faced by the Chestnut Plan leadership team in giving leadership to the implementation of the Plan and the neighborhood's overall revitalization. It also considers the contributions and hindrances to implementing the Plan. These considerations are offered to be instructive for other communities seeking transformation.

1

A Theology of Urban Ministry for Community Transformation

*C*ommunity or neighborhood transformation is about re-claiming prodigal communities, those communities that have strayed from God's purposes for them. Isaiah speaks of a time when the Root of Jesse, the Messiah, will reach out and reclaim the remnant of His people, bringing the outcasts home from the far corners of the earth and causing them to dwell peaceably in a safe place (*Isa. 11*). The involvement of the church, as the Messiah's representative, in revitalizing a community is about making it a safe place where all can live out God's purposes peaceably.

The theology of urban ministry that informs this reclamation effort is rooted in the theologies of place, peace, and prayer. These same theologies should form the basis for participation in community revitalization by any Christian or collection of Christians.

Theology of Place—the City as Context of Ministry

On September 11, 2001, the world was shocked and devastated by three terrorist attacks perpetrated against the United States in New York City, in Washington, D.C., and near Pittsburgh, Penn., that resulted in the deaths of thousands of people. The president of the United States reacted by stating, "Today, our nation saw evil." His statement suggested that this magnitude of evil had not been seen before, at least not in our lifetimes.

In October 2002, the Washington, D.C., metropolitan area came under siege. It was terrorized by two snipers, who randomly killed ten people and wounded three others in public places in about three weeks.

Indeed, almost daily, any urban newspaper will provide reports of evil and human conflict raising their heads in cities. Jeremiah emphasized a similar theme as God looked through his eyes at the cities of Jerusalem and Judah in Jeremiah 9:11–14:

> *I will make Jerusalem a heap of ruins, a haunt of jackals; and I will lay waste the towns of Judah so no one can live there…*

> *The LORD said, "It is because they have forsaken my law, which I set before them; they have not obeyed me or followed my law. Instead, they have followed the stubbornness of their hearts; they have followed the Baals, as their fathers taught them."*

As I look at Austin, Texas, the city in which I live and do ministry, I am stricken by its positive and negative attributes that coincide with those of biblical cities. Much about Austin is positive and many of its inhabitants are righteous, but there is also idolatry, selfishness, violence, lies, exploitation, and injustice.

Since it is the capital of Texas, it is also a gathering place for people who seek political power.

As I walk among the disinherited, dispossessed, ethnic minorities, and poor people of the city, I hear their comments about governmental agencies, social and educational institutions, real estate developers, public officials, and police. It is as if these institutions are seen as evil enemies whose efforts are against the neighborhoods and the people of the city. Therefore, like other cities, Austin can be seen as a venue for on-going and active spiritual warfare. Nevertheless, Christians engaged in community transformation must seek to carry out Christ's mission to make disciples and develop liberated communities in the city.

Indeed, Christians cannot participate in neighborhood transformation without offering the gospel. If they do social outreach and fail to offer the good news of Jesus Christ, "they have failed to offer their best gift."[1] Participating in a neighborhood's transformation creates an opportunity to share the Christian faith because it builds relationships of trust between the people of the church and the people of the neighborhood. It is a way to live out the gospel, and once trust is established, the natural extension is to share the gospel.

One of the things that can be achieved through community transformation is a sense of community. Beginning with the book of Genesis, the Bible makes clear that all people of the world are interrelated and should live in community. With this understanding, all people should live together in mutual respect, caring for and being morally responsible to one another.

A biblical sense of community supports the notion that communities and neighborhoods are sacred because God is present and at work in them. Raymond J. Bakke asserts that there can be no throwaway real estate because,

> *"The earth is the LORD's, and everything in it."*
> *(Ps. 24:1)* [2]

However, a church cannot partner with or be a vital and contributing part of a neighborhood unless it loves the neighborhood, even though it is a venue for ongoing spiritual warfare. A church that is not involved in transforming its community gives strong evidence that it does not love its community and implies that it does not even want to be located in the community. Consequently, a church that wants to be in relationship with a neighborhood that is pursuing transformation must join the community in addressing the issues that confront it, with the recognition that the people of that neighborhood must take final responsibility for addressing those issues.

Nevertheless, there is value in a church participating in a neighborhood's transformation. Anecdotal accounts indicate that when a church that has been a part of a community considers moving its physical location from that community, neighborhood residents do not want it to leave. These sentiments suggest that there is a relationship between the presence and ministry of one or more churches and the preservation or transformation of a neighborhood. [3]

A church's involvement in neighborhood transformation can also offer liberation for the church and neighborhood. As Jesus spoke of His purpose, He said,

> *"The Spirit of the Lord is on me, because he has anointed me . . . to proclaim freedom for the prisoners" (Luke 4:18).*

As Jesus' disciples, we have a mandate to work with Him in liberating those who are captive—whether to sin, poverty, injustice, exploitation, or oppression by others. Consequently, it is my experience that when a congregation moves beyond itself into the community and sees the liberating impact of its efforts, a liberating spirit develops within the church and among its members. Similarly, through liberation the neighborhood is released to emit a sweet scent of freedom.

God created the city (Ezek. 16:1–14). God owns the city and its people (Ps. 24:1). God gave the city to humankind (Deut. 6:10–14). God dwells in the city (Ps. 48:1–8, 14; Ezek. 16:1–14). God works in and protects the city (Ps. 8). God's grace is shown in the city. [4]

God's relationship with and response to the biblical cities inform our understanding of the extent of God's love for the city. God's response to sin in Sodom and Gomorrah demonstrates that God still cares for the city, despite the evil found in it (Gen. 18:20-33). It shows that no city is beyond restoration, patience, and compassion. God's response to Nineveh and Babylon shows that idolatry, pride, and selfishness lead to God's judgment and wrath, but the city has the potential for God's redemption. God's response to Jerusalem's violence and rebellion shows His passion and love for the city. The city, therefore, is reflective of God's greatness. It emerges from God's common grace as "a result of the mercy and goodness of God richly distributed to all humankind." [5]

God willed systems[6] into existence for the good and well-being of His creation. [7] Consequently, "All cities have systems [that] . . . work together to ensure the common good, i.e., to nurture, to transport, to protect, to educate, to inform, and so on."[8] These systems were created to continue and keep the city from degenerating into chaos, given humanity's fallen condition.[9] When properly functioning, they keep humankind from self-destructing. However, these systems "have moral values embedded in them,"[10] so they can become sinful, distorted, corrupt, oppressive, and exploitative.[11]

The city takes on a distinctive personality and collective spirit based on "a combination of . . . history, surroundings, and systems, the people who have moved through it, and the events that have occurred in it."[12] Sociologist Emile Durkheim would call these aspects "social facts"—certain non-material realities that significantly influence the people in the city. His observation that a city, as a concentration of people, has an effervescence—a collective spirit or life of its own—that transcends the individual and emerges from the interaction of its inhabitants is persuasive. He notes:

> *Society is a reality sui generis; it has its own peculiar characteristics, which are not found elsewhere and which are not met again in the same form in all the rest of the universe. The representations which express it have a wholly different contents from purely individual ones and we may rest assured in advance that the first add something to the second. . . .*

> *Collective representations are the result of an immense co-operation, which stretches out not only into space but into time as well; to make them, a multitude of minds have associated, united and combined their ideas and sentiments; for them, long generations have accumulated their experience and their knowledge. A special intellectual activity is therefore concentrated in them which is infinitely richer and complexer than that of the individual.[13]*

Therefore, the social facts of a city result in a collective spirit that influences its inhabitants for good or evil.

When I reflect upon Birmingham, Alabama, the city in which I was raised during the 1950s and 1960s, I am convinced that it had a collective spirit that was evil. The unadulterated racism seen in the behavior of its white people and institutions leaves little doubt about the existence of personal, social, and institutional sin. Birmingham's history, surroundings, and systems, the people who moved through it, and the events that occurred in it combined to develop this collective evil spirit.

The city in which I now live, Austin, Texas, is the capital of Texas, the home of state politics, and the seat of the state's university system. The majority of state government employees live in the area. Austin has long been a "government town," where the main employers historically were governmental entities. One does not have to live in Austin long to discover that it is a city that values politics and learning. It is also now called a "City of Ideas," as demonstrated by its creative business ventures. As technology companies and other new businesses move into Austin and seek to become participating corporate citizens, it is interesting to observe how they "bounce against" the city's political environment.

Over the years, I have become increasingly aware that these aspects of Austin have led to a collective spirit whose profile is power, politics, ideas, and territorialism, and these influences are reflected on Austin's inhabitants, institutions, systems, and churches. This spirit also can be seen in personal and social relationships. My experiences and observations, therefore, convince me that a city and its neighborhoods have collective spirits that influence the attitudes and actions of its people and systems.

The city's systems and collective spirit have come under attack from principalities and powers, demonic powers that are at work to oppress them.[14] The Apostle Paul describes the situation this way: "For our struggle is not against flesh and flood, but against the rulers, against the authorities, against the powers of this dark world and against the spiritual forces of evil in the heavenly realms" (Eph. 6:12).

These principalities and powers are very real forces, even if they cannot be easily defined.[15] Although created by God through Christ (Col. 1:15–17) for the good of God's creation and to serve God's purposes,[16] they have been captured by Satan and are now oppressing creation (1 Cor. 2:8; Eph. 2:1–3; Col. 2:8, 20–22).[17] They have a dominant influence on people and systems. "They are fallen 'powers' with idolatrous-demonic claims."[18] They influence the city's systems and collective spirit. They can damage the city's soul.

People in the city influence the city's systems and collective spirit, and the systems and collective spirit influence the people. In a sense, people in cities are responsible for the moral conduct of one another (Deut. 22:15). They do not function independently of one another. They can influence for good or evil.

What happens in the city also affects surrounding geographical areas. The effects go outward like concentric circles. Based on Ezekiel 16, Bakke suggests that cities are family systems, with the suburbs as children of the city.[19] Many years ago, evangelist Dwight L. Moody "recognized the cities as the centers of national life."[20]

When sin accumulates among people, the city itself becomes overwhelmed and possessed by sin because of this interrelatedness (Gen. 19). The whole city is affected by any part, and all must suffer the consequences (Deut. 13:15–16). [21] The sin takes on corporate dimensions because a large number of the city's inhabitants indulge in it (Isa. 58:3–7; 59:12–14).[22] Consequently, there is a systemic relationship between the occupants of a city, its systems and institutions, and the surrounding communities. As sin corrupts and takes control of city dwellers like poison, the collective spirit of the city or geographical area is infected and

people will likely join groups and churches where there is affirmation, caring, and fellowship. Communities of *koinonia*, therefore, are effective vehicles for sharing Jesus' good news.

I have found in my ministry that there is a fear among God's people about sharing the good news of Jesus Christ, even in existing relationships. There seems to be an uncertainty about what to say. There also seems to be some reservation about sharing the message of Jesus because people realize their actions are sometimes inconsistent with the message. Some also seem to reminiscence about their previous carnal life, what they used to do before accepting Jesus Christ, and feel some embarrassment about speaking to others about their lives and need for Jesus.

Accordingly, the church I pastor decided to utilize an evangelistic model that helps our members learn how to share the gospel through relationships and social contacts. This model emphasizes that "success is more than leading someone to Christ. Success is living the Christian life day by day, sharing the gospel, and trusting God for the results. Success is not bringing someone to Christ."[40] Through this emphasis, we have learned that it takes more than the message of peace to communicate the good news; it also requires the practice of peace. The way God's people relate to people in relationships is an important factor in who and what the church claims to be. Through this type of sharing, our cities are being transformed one relationship at a time.

Paul also presents *koinonia* through the church sharing grace (Phil. 1:7). The early church sent the message that although all people have sinned and fallen short of the glory of God (Rom. 3:23), God's grace (His unmerited favor and love) was available through Jesus Christ.

When Jesus was on earth, He had relationships with people who were on the fringes of life—unloved and rejected people—

who needed God's grace. The church in the city today needs to be the presence of grace that is extended to all people. The church's message that "God so loved the world" (John 3:16) must be consistent with methods of love as demonstrated through acts of grace.

Philip Yancey suggests that the world runs by "ungrace" and believes that the world cannot offer grace because it insists that we earn our way.[41] Sadly, he notes: "I rejected the church for a time because I found so little grace there. I returned because I found grace nowhere else."[42] Such an assessment makes the flow of grace through the church all the more strategic, since "grace is Christianity's best gift to the world."[43]

On one occasion, Dr. Gardner Taylor, a retired prominent New York City pastor, was asked what he perceived to be the critically unique business of the church that distinguished it from all other institutions. He said, "the business of the church is to present the souls of believers at the throne of grace with the reasonable assurance that they will be found acceptable."[44]

His strategy for accomplishing that objective was to be "a good role model." The gift of grace can also be demonstrated as God's people act as good role models.

Grace also can be conveyed through acts of compassion. It can be practiced by individuals through their actions and by churches through ministries that are designed to meet the needs of people inside and outside the church. People who are loved and nurtured by God's people are more likely to be receptive to the influence of the good news of God's peace. The church that has an open-door policy for all people who need this message will go a long way toward participating in transforming the city.

As God's people work toward transforming the city and community through need-based ministries of grace, acts of compassion, and outreach, they will see lives transformed inside and outside the church. I believe such acts of *koinonia* that share grace declare more about one's relationship with Christ and one's interest in the neighborhood than words can convey.

Another way to experience the fellowship found in *koinonia* is created and informed by the Holy Spirit (Phil. 2:1). People are looking for and are impressed by the kind of authentic relationships that can be experienced in a *koinonia* community that is shaped and influenced by the fruit of the Spirit, which is

> *"love, joy, peace, patience, kindness, generosity, faithfulness, gentleness, and self-control"*
> *(Gal. 5:22–23).*

> *The Spirit's fruit are…marks of genuine spirituality. The Spirit seeks to restore the fellowship broken by sin and to overcome the separation in a bond of love.* [45]

In *koinonia*, people can experience these qualities in fellowship and be spiritually formed by the Spirit. Experiencing and being shaped by the Spirit can only lead to transforming the city into a place for peace. But we must be mindful that the mission of the church is to seek the peace of God (Col. 3:15), and the Holy Spirit seeks to maintain the "bond of peace" (Eph. 4:3) through relationships that result in beneficial social consequences for individuals and systems. Thus, the message in a koinonia community must be clear:

> *"the mind controlled by the Spirit is life and peace"*
> *(Romans 8:6).*

Perhaps that is why C. Norman Kraus concludes that "the Spirit's power furnishes a new possibility for peace to be realized in the community."[46]

Koinonia also involves suffering (Phil. 3:10), which is an intimate part of life in the city in the context of the on-going battle between good and evil. People and systems can mistreat, exploit, and harm people in the city.

Theologian Howard Thurman notes,

> *The masses of men live with their backs constantly against the wall. They are the poor, the disinherited, the dispossessed. What does our religion say to them? The issue is not what it counsels them to do for others whose need may be greater, but what religion offers to meet their own needs.*[47]

In the midst of confusion about the unfairness of life and the love of God, bad things happen to good people, and the peace that God desires for people can be fleeting or absent if they believe He is not fair or just. Hence, a fundamental question for people who suffer is, "What does the church offer to meet our needs?" In an effort to answer that question, the church must be engaged in suffering so that its response of *koinonia* can be properly processed through the lens of the good news of peace through Jesus Christ. Through suffering, *koinonia* lives, and systems can be redeemed and transformed for peaceful living even in the midst of suffering.

Scripture places a heavy emphasis on suffering for others as a calling for the people of God (e.g., James 1:1–4). Like Jesus Christ, His followers must be willing to suffer for the good of others and the spreading of the good news of peace.

It has been observed that there is a price to pay for the church being in partnership with the hurting, the needy, the disinherited, the poor, and the oppressed in its midst, because it is a partnership with the suffering of the cross.[48]

> *Ultimately—for Paul as for ourselves—we cannot really enter into a true Koinonia/fellowship (a partnership of sharing in his suffering with others) if we have not and if we do not experience his resurrection power.* [49]

The essence of this type of partnership in suffering is that the people of God must be willing to confront individuals and systems that do not honor the image of God in humankind. The church must be willing to speak truth to power on behalf of the poor, the needy, the disinherited, the rejected, and the mistreated.

As part of being in a transformation partnership with a disenfranchised community, God's people occasionally will find themselves confronting institutions, governmental and business leaders, and entities on behalf of the poor, the children, and the mistreated. While it will not always be a comfortable experience, it is essential for God's people, as suffering partners in koinonia, to demonstrate a prophetic witness in the city. [50]

The church must walk among the people of the city, hear their needs, see how they are oppressed by evil, advocate on their behalf, and offer ministries in the name of Jesus. The suffering that will accompany this walk is simply a part of the "partnership with the crucified God"[51] because "living the gospel means sharing in the suffering and pain of others."[52]

Not too long ago, my hometown experienced a terrible flood, with more than six hundred homes and businesses being devastated. People were in need of clothing and homes were in need of repair. The religious community was called upon to respond in a coordinated effort to provide disaster relief.

One response of Christians could have been to declare that:

> *"Jesus is Lord and God raised Him from the dead. Be comforted in Him."*

But is that really good news to the homeowner, family, or business owner who has been displaced and suffered loss because of a flood? Ministering to immediate needs provides an opportunity to demonstrate God's peace in a tangible way. These tragedies gave God's people the opportunity to demonstrate their commitment to community through sharing economic resources or economic *koinonia* (2 Cor. 8:1–7; Phil. 4:14–15). Although not all of the people who experienced the flood devastation were Christians, such an opportunity is nevertheless reminiscent of the early church, where

> *"All the believers were together and had everything in common. Selling their possessions and goods, they gave to anyone as he had need"* (Acts 2:44–45).

Sharing our economic resources with others demonstrates our interrelatedness as a community, models the kingdom of God for the city, and presents an opportunity to transform the city through relationships.

The task of the church is to represent Christ in the heart of the city.[53] We must love people. Closely tied to this mission are acts of neighborly love through ministries of peace.

The biblical parable of the good Samaritan (Luke 10:30–37) teaches that the ministry of Christians must extend to each needy person whom God makes our neighbor. The book of Jonah also challenges God's people to go beyond their comfort zones and boundaries to love the people God loves.

It is also important to love with compassion. Throughout the recorded life of Jesus, He spoke and acted with compassion. In our communities and neighborhoods, Christians also are to act with compassion. But we often want to be detached to avoid the pain, trouble, and afflictions we encounter.

This demonstration of love requires *diakonia*, or ministries of peace to a broken and hurting humanity. It also requires being the salt of the earth and the light of the world in the city. As an example, my congregation's vision statement says:

> David Chapel Missionary Baptist Church should be a prayerful, loving and tithing church with a heart for the community that shows its love for Christ by offering God's hospitality, hope and healing to its members and beyond.

This statement urges us to develop and implement ministries of peace in our community to the glory of God. Jesus' words instruct us as to the attitude we must have when we act:

> "Not so with you. Instead, whoever wants to become great among you must be your servant, and whoever wants to be first must be slave of all. For even the Son of Man did not come to be served, but to serve, and to give his life as a ransom for many." (Mark 10:43–45)

The people of God should serve as agents of peace (i.e., reconciliation, welfare, and justice).[54] Words (Isa. 8:20) and actions (Eph. 5:8) are essential if we are to have ministries of peace through which we sprinkle salt and shine light (Matt. 5:13–16). Accordingly, our ministries must live out this spirit of peace. But in establishing ministries of peace, the church must be cognizant of God's preference for the poor (Matt. 11:1-6; 1 Cor. 1:26–31; James 2:5).[55] Such a preference teaches that encounters with the poor lead to encounters with the Lord.[56]

In developing ministries of peace, particularly for the poor, it is helpful to consider a suggested typology for social diakonia, based on the Chinese proverb, "To Give a Fish."[57] It is not unusual to find one of these types dominating a church's approach to ministries of peace, although all these approaches have some value.

If the city and its inhabitants are to be transformed and empowered, pursuing social education, social development, and social justice should be primary focuses of the church's ministries. This means the church must get serious about issues such as racial conflict and relations, education, health care, employment, economic opportunities, housing, injustice, and oppression overall. It means political engagement in these issues, as well as working to ensure that peace permeates the city so that God is honored. But we must also know our city and identify its collective spirit so that we can partner in transforming the city by developing ministries of peace that address the needs of that city.

One of the ways my congregation has attempted to develop ministries of peace has been to engage in surveys of both the surrounding neighborhood and our church membership. Walking the neighborhood and talking and listening to people have helped us to know the personal and social needs of the people. We have had numerous meetings with neighborhood residents and set up a neighborhood-church planning team to develop a neighborhood revitalization plan for neighborhood approval. We also recognized the need to connect people with available social and governmental services.

Tom Skinner makes an interesting observation:

> *One of the things that keeps the church from being a voice in the community is that the Church doesn't do the things of God in locations where the world will be able to see it. Most Christians reserve*

> *all of their teaching and preaching and testifying for one another.* [58]

The church in the city must come out of the catacombs and be a voice in the community so that people can hear and see the message of God's peace.

Through ministries of peace, God's people must be participants in Christ's transformative and redemptive mission. This was the secret of the early church's explosive power[59] and can be the source of the church's power today. We should never forget that God, the source of our power, is also present in the city.

Since God is present in the city, the church must confess, celebrate, and worship the Prince of Peace. In a sense, the city becomes "holy ground" where Jesus Christ is worshiped:

> *In worship, we see ourselves as the people of God, motivated to the service we are instructed to render. If the conscience of the world is to be moved by the conscience of Christ, it must come through the God-consciousness of the church penetrating the world.* [60]

But worship of God is an antagonistic act of war that confronts the principalities and powers that are at work to oppose God. At its core, worship is about engaging in spiritual warfare. The principalities and powers want humankind's allegiance, while worship of God focuses on exclusive allegiance to Him. Worship is inextricably connected with how one lives and seeks to bring human life under control of the Prince of Peace. Worship should influence the daily living of all who worship. Each act of worship should yield a new commitment to God. It should motivate God's people to be servants and to share their resources that come from God. It should inspire witnessing, because worship reminds worshipers of God's redemptive acts on behalf of humankind.

The people of God can make a difference in a community by how they worship through their lives (Prov. 10:21; 11:10–11). Indeed, godly living in a city can militate against the influence and corruption of sin.

A part of worship, therefore, is discipleship. As God's people live lives of worship, participate in community transformation, and share the gospel through relationships of trust, they will have opportunities to minister to people who have real needs. One should be able to engage in discipling, which "is the process by which a person is changed at the deepest level of his being so that both his inner and his outer life reflect the redemptive (saving and sanctifying) impact of Jesus Christ."[61] Notably, one observer of urban ministry has asserted that discipling "must include both the spiritual transformation of persons and the social transformation of places."[62] Transforming a community is the process of socially transforming a place, while sharing the gospel is the process of spiritually transforming a person.

My congregation has attempted to keep the worship of Jesus Christ in the forefront of our community-transformation efforts. We see our neighborhood as "holy ground," and our worship of God motivates us to serve Him in our community.

In our neighborhood, my congregation's worship is seen through its involvement in community gatherings, participation in community initiatives and groups, and service on committees and task forces that address issues in the city. Our worship is seen through regular appearances before government officials on issues of public concern. It is seen through meetings with business leaders regarding economic development and opportunities for poor and low-income people. It is seen through our use of our human and financial resources to uplift the community. Through our worship, we call attention to the Prince of Peace as

His partners in transforming our city.

Theology of Prayer—the City and Spirituality

Prayer is dangerous because it, like worship, confronts the principalities and powers. Eldin Villafañe asserts, "The church's mission must include confronting and dismantling the claims of the 'dominion of death' in the city. This 'dominion of death' must be confronted above all by prayer."[63] In a sense, whether or not a city is transformed depends upon prayer. Jesus said,

> *"Ask the Lord of the harvest, therefore, to send out workers into his harvest field" (Matt. 9:38),*

which suggests that much of the harvest might be lost if the people of God do not pray. In commenting on Ephesians 6:12–20, Clinton E. Arnold says:

> *"If Paul were to summarize the primary way of gaining access to the power of God for waging successful spiritual warfare, he would unwaveringly affirm that it is through prayer. Prayer is given much greater prominence in the spiritual warfare passage than any of the other implements."[64]*

Prayer is an offensive weapon in spiritual warfare.

It is important that a partnership between God's people and a community recognize the need and urgency of prayer. God's people must understand that their efforts to revitalize and transform the neighborhood are resulting in spiritual battle. They also must understand that they must be unified. They must recognize that they are dealing with a collective spirit and systems that are beyond their ability to affect. As with Nehemiah, they must recognize the value of praying for their community (Neh.1:4–11). My congregation's vision prayer says in part,

> *God our Father, speak to us as we pray... Let our hearts and spirits know how we, individually and as a church, can be the salt of the earth and the lights of the world in this community. May our lights so shine before men, women, boys and girls that they may see Your Son lifted up, our good works and glorify You.*

By regularly praying for their community, God's people are continually reminded of their task and mission. In fact, their prayers can motivate and inform their ministry efforts. But a likely result will be that God will bring to the church, as members, disinherited and oppressed people who challenge our proclamation to be consistent with our actions. Therefore, we must embrace Kenneth Leech's observation about the Holy Spirit:

> *He is the Spirit of the Age to Come, the initiator of a new order where young men shall see visions and old men shall dream dreams. Prayer which lacks this future orientation is bound to become settled and at ease, a victim of that false peace against which the prophets constantly warn us.*[65]

Our desire should not be to have that false peace. Our prayers, therefore, become cries for the kingdom and for God to work in our community and city. It is only through God's power that the city can be redeemed and transformed.

Conclusion

In a recent National Geographic article, a journalist asked a West African teacher what would become of his city, "Djenne—Eternal City of West Africa," as he considered its future after years of drought and decay. He replied:

> *Many say Djenne is going to lose its value, that people are going to leave. But Djenne will be well inhabited as before. Djenne of the future is Djenne of the past. Djenne's future—its survival—depends on its ability to hold to the essentials of its past. It adapts to changing circumstances while guarding what lasts. This is the city's ultimate power, its* nyama, *if you will—that it endures.*[66]

As with Djenne, the city of the future is the city of the past. After years of spiritual drought and decay, the city's future depends, to a large extent, on the church's willingness to partner with God in pursuing and holding to God's created essentials—the city as a peaceful place with no injustice, crime, poverty, or disease, until the well-inhabited "New Jerusalem," the truly eternal and peace-full city, comes down from heaven. Let us pray the church will take this journey to reclaim our prodigal communities.

2

Approaches to Community Transformation

I am persuaded that a singularly effective way of facilitating the transformation of a community and city is the application of the concept of systems thinking to Christian theology and ministry. It should take place within the context of the participation of God's people in transforming a community. In other words, God's people should be involved with the community in a process in which all partners are learning how to transform the community, recognizing that it is interrelated with and interdependent on other entities and individuals.

The application of systems thinking to theology has been called "systemic theology" by Douglas and Judy Hall.[1] Peter Senge has noted that "systems thinking" is a conceptual framework and an amorphous body of knowledge, methods, and tools that has developed over more than fifty years to help show how business and other human endeavors, such as learning organizations, are interrelated systems and part of a common process. It is an approach to facilitate the art and practice of collective learning. Because community revitalization is always about an interconnected system, any person involved in such an effort will benefit from using systems thinking as a developmental and evaluative framework.

Notably, this approach includes five disciplines: systems thinking, personal mastery, mental models, building shared vision, and team learning.

The discipline of systems thinking is an approach to understanding the interconnectedness of social reality. It looks at segments of a social reality as a whole system rather than as individual and disconnected segments. As an example, Senge observes, "You can only understand the system of a rainstorm by contemplating the whole, not any individual part of the pattern."[2] David McCamus notes that systems principles call for

> *"peripheral vision: the ability to pay attention to the world as if through a wide-angle, not a tele-photo lens, so you can see how your actions inter-relate with other areas of activity."*[3]

Since a community transformation effort is collaborative and involves many participants, systems thinking is particularly useful in assessing its progress. It is tempting for any partner to lose sight of the fact that revitalization is taking place among connected parts of the community. Systems thinking, therefore, can help the effort remain balanced and on target.

Senge defines *personal mastery* as:

> *[The] discipline of continually clarifying and deepening our personal vision, of focusing our ener-gies, or developing patience, and of seeing reality objectively. As such, it is an essential cornerstone of the learning organization—the learning organiza-tion's spiritual foundation.*[4]

It has been said that

> *"the central practice of personal mastery involves learning to keep both a personal vision and a clear picture of current reality before us. . . . Personal mastery teaches us not to lower our vision."*[5]

Hence, the people of a community can learn to practice personal mastery by continuing to discuss their vision for their community and by assessing the matters that help and hinder the vision's accomplishment.

Mental models are "the images, assumptions, and stories which we carry in our minds of ourselves, other people, institutions, and every aspect of the world."[6] An exciting aspect of a community-transformation initiative can be the opportunity to candidly share and assess the mental models of the participants. These conversations and discussions can allow the participants to develop a shared vision.

Building shared vision "involves the skills of unearthing shared 'pictures of the future' that foster genuine commitment and enrollment rather than compliance."[7] Indeed, a significant challenge to the partnership could be the need to recognize that building a shared vision is a never-ending process. But the implementation of the vision must remain consistent with the shared vision. The transformation effort requires continual self-regulation, and systems thinking is essential to its effectiveness.

Team learning is the process by which members of a team develop the capacity "to think and act in new synergistic ways, with full coordination and a sense of unity, because team members know each other's hearts and minds . . . they develop the capacity to use their disagreements to make their collective understanding richer."[8] The community must continually learn to engage in team learning.

According to Douglas and Judy Hall, systems thinking nurtures a learning environment

> *"that ultimately can help an individual or a group of persons be in tune with God's infinitely broad and long-term plan, and thus a part of His redemptive process in our world. . . . The purpose of systemic theology is to see God's truth in its natural interrelated nature. . . . The Bible—written when world culture still operated at a more primary cultural level—unvaryingly supports the idea of seeing people, cities, and countries as whole interrelated and interdependent systems. . . . A systemic approach to theology and ministry is encapsulated in [community, redemptive, and high calling].*[9]

In addressing the application of systems thinking to the urban church, the Halls make a distinction between urban ministries that use *program action* and those that use *system action*. Program action uses a problem-solving approach to urban issues. *System action* recognizes that urban issues take place within a system, where they are constantly interacting with each other and are constantly being acted upon by outside dynamics that are constantly changing.

> *Program action follows conscious thought. System action, however, is too complex for conscious thought alone, and springs from intuitive or subconscious thought. Effective urban ministers cannot always clearly explain—in the usual logical ways—how they minister. This is because they often use subconscious thinking. They don't always know*

*why they do things, they just do them! And things
"turn out right!"[10]*

*As urban ministry practitioners, we need to
move from system action to systems thinking. If we
do not thus learn to apprehend our actions through
systems thinking, we will most likely drift from intuitive systems action to program action.[11]*

For the urban practitioner, systems thinking is an intentional
process by which to understand the operation of an urban system.

Notably, systems thinking can aid one's understanding of
systemic dimensions of community transformation in general
and the revitalization or transformation of a certain community
in particular. It can make one aware of the complex socio-
political-religious systemic aspects of a community that can help
and hinder transformation. It also gives one tools to understand
these aspects. Indeed, effective and sustained community
transformation cannot be realized without knowledge and
awareness of the interrelated systems of a community and the
strategies that facilitate the transformation process. Therefore,
any community transformation undertaking, whether partnering
with a church or not, must necessarily involve collaboration
within the context of that community's system. Yet in order
to understand how systemic theology engages the church in
community transformation, there are some theological issues,
such as the intersection of Christ and culture and the church
and its urban mission that must be considered.

Christ and Culture

Any person interested in understanding how the church should interface with its culture or city, whether through community transformation or in some other way, must familiarize himself or herself with H. Richard Niebuhr's classic book, *Christ and Culture*. Niebuhr reviews the recurring arguments about how Christians should relate to their culture and notes the following:

> *In this situation it is helpful to remember that the question of Christianity and civilization is by no means a new one; that Christian perplexity in this area has been perennial, and that the problem has been an enduring one through all the Christian centuries. It is helpful also to recall that the repeated struggles of Christians with this problem have yielded no single Christian answer, but only a series of typical answers which together, for faith, represent phases of the strategy of the militant church in the world. That strategy, however, being in the mind of the Captain rather than of any lieutenants, is not under the control of the latter. Christ's answer to the problem of human culture is one thing, Christian answers are another; yet his followers are assured that he uses their various works in accomplishing his own. . . . The belief which lies back of this effort, however, is the conviction that Christ as living Lord is answering the question in the totality of history and life in a fashion which transcends the wisdom of all his interpreters yet employs their partial insights and their necessary conflicts.* [12]

Accordingly, Niebuhr identifies five different perspectives on the church in its culture: Christ against culture, Christ of culture, Christ above culture, Christ and culture in paradox, and Christ: the transformer of culture. He observes "culture" as the "'artificial, secondary environment' which man superimposes on the natural. It comprises language, habits, ideas, beliefs, customs, social organization, inherited artifacts, technical processes, and values."[13] A Christian's view of the role of the church in the culture of the city, therefore, will affect how and to what extent one does ministry in attempting to transform a community.

Christ against culture "uncompromisingly affirms the sole authority of Christ over the Christian and resolutely rejects culture's claims to loyalty."[14] Christ is seen as opposed to society's customs and human achievement, and He confronts us with an "either-or" decision.[15] Christians who adopt this perspective will not become involved with their culture because "it is in culture that sin chiefly resides."[16] Therefore, they will not engage in a collaborative approach to transforming a community because then they would be engaged with sinful culture.

Niebuhr notes that the Christ against culture view has had historical importance while not being an adequate perspective. He observes, "Christian withdrawals from and rejections of the institutions of society . . . have led to reformations in both church and world."[17] Although withdrawal and renunciation play a vital part in every Christian's life, in this perspective there are other theological considerations that argue against this position. Indeed, the Christian must participate in "parabolic actions" that provide signs of God's activity within culture and the world.[18]

The *Christ of culture* perspective is embraced by Christians who "seek to maintain community with all other believers. Yet they seem equally at home in the community of culture. They feel no great tension between church and world. . . . On the one hand they interpret culture through Christ . . . on the other hand they understand Christ through culture."[19] To Christians who relate to culture in this way,

> *Jesus often appears as a great hero of human culture history; his life and teachings are regarded as the greatest human achievement; in him, it is believed, the aspirations of men toward their values are brought to a point of culmination; he confirms what is best in the past, and guides the process of civilization to its proper goal. Moreover, he is a part of culture in the sense that he himself is part of the social heritage that must be transmitted and conserved.[20]*

For the Christ of culture proponent, Niebuhr observes, "Christ is identified with what men conceive to be their finest ideals, their noblest institutions, and their best philosophy." [21] Participating in community transformation would not present a conflict to a Christ of culture Christian.

The Christian who adopts the *Christ above culture* view "affirms both Christ and culture, as one who confesses a Lord who is both of this world and of the other." [22] In offering biblical support for this perspective, Niebuhr points to Matthew 22:21 and Romans 13:1, 6.[23] Niebuhr admittedly uses these verses as not directly on point or expressive of this view, but argues that they "sound the motif." [24] These verses, however, seem to support the position that God is not above the culture but of this world. They simply do not speak to God's "other worldliness;" rather, they speak of the Christian's obligations to God in this world.

The *Christ and culture in paradox* perspective is held by the dualist, who has a conflict "between the righteousness of God and the righteousness of self."[25] One who is obedient to God must also be obedient to Christ, who judges society; obedient to the institutions of society; and loyal to its members.[26]

> *As long as man remains in the body he has need*
> *then, it seems, of a culture and of the institutions of*
> *culture not because they advance him toward life*
> *with Christ but because they restrain wickedness in*
> *a sinful and temporal world.*[27]

The *Christ: the transformer of culture* perspective is similar to the Christ and culture in paradox perspective, "but it also has affinities with the other great Christian attitudes."[28] Christ converts men and women in their culture and society. In expounding on this perspective Charles Scriven says, "Through Christ God seeks to renew the human world—now corrupted but in principle good because he has made it and has pronounced it good."[29] The Christian who engages in community transformation fundamentally affirms that culture and the city must be confronted because culture and the city affect people, institutions, and systems. In other words, the Christian who embraces this perspective would participate in community transformation as an approach to transforming the culture and city.

I do not believe the church should be against the city or culture, because they are not its enemies. The church should not be of the city or culture, because it can lose its prophetic voice and compromise its spiritual authority and redemptive responsibilities to speak to the culture. The church should not be above or aloof from the city or culture, because it then will be isolated and have no impact on the city or culture. But one could say that the city is a creature of God that has gone astray.

Therefore, I am of the view that the church must engage in a confrontation with and transformation of the city or culture. In order for a community to be transformed and reclaimed for the intended purposes of God, the church must be a participant. But it is essential that those who participate in this effort have a shared vision as to what the community must look like after it has been transformed.

Such is the advantage of a collaborative community plan that articulates this vision. When one knows how the transformed community should look, it is easier to know when transformation has been achieved. Therefore, I am persuaded of the need for neighborhood plans with strategies that correspond to specific geographical boundaries of areas that are perceived to be in need of transformation. Such neighborhood plans are essential to effective and sustained neighborhood transformation.

Community transformation is a just social cause in which the church must be involved. And the church should work in collaboration with others in a community and should participate in or facilitate organizing the community to seek justice or social change. It is clear to me that both are essential in order for a church to work toward revitalizing a community.

Eldin Villafañe has effectively challenged Christians about the need to engage and approach, rather than flee from, the issues of the city through a "social spirituality."[30] Relying on Jeremiah 29:5–7, Villafañe describes the "Jeremiah Paradigm for the City," which he says describes the role of the church (God's people) in the city today. He argues convincingly that the church and its members must "struggle and live in the city" by being present in the city with a sense of mission or ministry that embraces an authentic, relevant, and wholistic spirituality that is actively demonstrated in a social context through love for God and one another. In other words, Villafañe argues,

> *"The brokenness of society (so visible in the barrios and ghettos of our cities), the scriptural missional mandate, and the Spirit's love constrain us to feed the hungry, visit the sick and prisoners, shelter the homeless and poor—to express God's love in social concerns. We do this as an expression of faithful obedience and authentic spirituality."* [31]

The Church's Urban Mission

It is interesting how churches have thought about cities and ministered in cities in the United States since World War II.[32] A church engaged in community revitalization may be acting as an independent congregation or as a part of a denominational strategy. There are some common features of the urban ministry approaches undertaken by congregations and denominations. Denominations are concerned about large groups of people that make up national and international constituencies. They have oversight for clergy development and education. They engage large systems and structures because of their national and international reach. They have concerns about national patterns and trends. They keep watch over their unique heritage, principles, and values. Their resources have to address local, national, and international concerns. Denominational priorities also often preempt local priorities.

Denominations are not as informed about local issues as are congregations. Their ability to engage or identify local issues, systems, structures, and institutions is limited. Sometimes the denomination itself becomes a system that needs to be confronted by the congregation that seeks to be effective in community revitalization.

Congregations generally give greater ministry emphasis to local issues, but can be narrow-minded or blinded to systemic issues that need to be addressed by urban ministry beyond the local context. They are better able than denominations to understand the local context and implications of urban and community issues. They generally engage local systems and structures. They are able to mobilize local volunteers and resources to address local urban challenges. While they (particularly small congregations) are likely to be collaborative in their approaches, they may deemphasize broader national, international, and denominational issues because of their emphasis on local concerns. The temptation for the congregation is to be "local-focused" and not have a "kingdom-wide" perspective on urban ministry. Perhaps a systems approach to community revitalization could help militate against this potential for imbalance. Equally important for a congregation sincerely interested in revitalizing and ministering to its neighborhoods is collaboration and a shared vision that meets the needs of the neighborhoods.

Some denominations may consider their principal urban mission to "humanize the impersonal, individualized, and materialistic character of modern city life"[33] rather than to transform the city. Other denominations may struggle to define their constituency, values, and priorities.[34] Notably, although collaboration is to be highly valued in transforming a community, it has been argued that church leaders who plan and direct a church's work to realize effective urban church ministry must possess four attributes:

1) sociological awareness of the ministry context,

2) theological understanding of the church,

3) psychological insight about people, and

4) practical skills to plan and execute plans. [35]

Holy Change

3

A Systemic Experiment: Revitalizing the Chestnut Neighborhood in Austin, Texas

Historical Context of Austin, Texas

*A*ustin, the capital city of Texas, was planned at the juncture of Shoal Creek and the Colorado River in 1838-39 by Mirabeau Buonaparte Lamar, the second elected president of Texas. The city is named after Stephen F. Austin, often referred to as the Father of Texas, who founded the first American colony in Texas in the 1820s.

In its first year, almost a thousand people moved to the city. Although President Sam Houston later removed the government to Houston, Austinites prevented the removal of the archives by force of arms, which may have saved the town's future.[1] In 1846, President Anson Jones returned the government to Austin. By 1860, Austin was connected to the state's major population centers by a system of established roadways, but it remained fairly isolated until the railroad arrived in 1871. Subsequently, Huston-Tillotson University (1876), the University of Texas main campus (1883), St. Edward's University (1885), Austin Presbyterian Theological Seminary (1902), Concordia University (1926, a Lutheran institution), the Episcopal Seminary of the Southwest (1952), and the Austin Graduate School of Theology, formerly the Institute for Christian Studies (1975, associated with the Churches of Christ), were located in Austin, and it became known as a college town in addition to being the state capital. Consequently, politics and education or ideas have historically permeated Austin's history.

Austin has become a global city, and the metropolitan area population far exceeds one million people. Now called a "city of ideas," Austin is part of a group of cities that is driven by a new productive force— "the creative class," as identified by Richard Florida.[2]

The people in this new class are inventive, creative, and imaginative workers who design computer software, compose songs, and write stories. These people make their livings by finding problems and solving them. They are in the business of producing new ideas, and the cities are the country's centers of growth and commercial innovation. By 2000, only Washington, D.C., Raleigh-Durham, N.C., Seattle, and San Francisco rank higher than Austin for concentration of creative workers among the fifty largest cities in the United States.[3] Boston, New York, Portland, and San Diego had smaller percentages of workers in creative jobs.[4]

Most of the nation's software and high-tech goods and services are produced in these cities, where most new ideas are patented. The economies of these cities are the most vigorous in the country. Consequently, these communities are welcoming places for both creative workers and foreign-born residents.

These trends are reflected in Austin. From 1990 to 2000, Austin added 85,097 foreign-born people to its population, or nearly 56 percent of the 152,834 foreign-born people who lived there as of March 2000. Many of these foreign-born residents were drawn by the technology industry, and are highly skilled and educated. Accordingly, many of the indigenous Austin residents have to compete with these individuals for jobs in this new creative economy.[5] Nevertheless, it has been said that such immigrants "revitalize the regions they move to and enrich them culturally with their tastes in music, food and entertainment."[6]

The cities of ideas are contrasted with "traditional cities" or those with "old economies," such as my hometown of Birmingham, Alabama. These traditional cities and their residents display the following characteristics:

- More likely to attend church
- More active in clubs, churches, volunteer services and civic projects
- More family-oriented
- More feelings of isolation
- More feelings of economic vulnerability
- Community projects increasing
- Political interest decreasing
- More supportive of traditional authority
- More sedentary
- Higher stress
- Poverty rates 50 percent higher
- More social activities with other people.[7]

By contrast, sociologist Robert Cushing says residents in cities of ideas like Austin have the following characteristics:

- Church attendance is decreasing
- More interested in other cultures and places
- More likely to "try anything once"
- More likely to engage in individualistic activities
- More optimistic
- Greater interest in politics
- More artists, musicians, and writers
- More gay couples
- Volunteerism is increasing, but less than in "old economy" cities
- Community projects decreasing more
- Club membership decreasing[8]

Notably, Austin residents have the following characteristics when compared to other cities of ideas:

- Church attendance lower
- Club attendance higher but less frequent
- Less supportive of traditional authority
- Less family-oriented
- Less feelings of isolation
- More likely to engage in individualistic activities
- Higher levels of trust
- Lower frequency of volunteering
- Less feelings of economic vulnerability
- More optimistic

- Less sedentary
- Less stress[9]

Many people in technology cities such as Austin are fashioning their own faiths through multiple traditions.[10] These growth dynamics for cities of ideas have implications for community transformation, and they present opportunities for outreach and ministries by Austin churches in particular. Indeed, many of the new arrivals to Austin experience anomie or a feeling of lostness, and need communities and relationships that will make them comfortable in their new setting.

These characteristics of Austin's residents present opportunities and challenges for community transformation, highlighting the need for more creative and relevant outreach strategies. In an effort to build community among the residents, neighborhoods could host block parties; ethnic festivals such as Juneteenth, Cinco de Mayo, and Chinese New Year; and community festivals during the seasons of the year surrounding Halloween and Christmas. It could also be valuable to promote a community policing partnership with the Austin Police Department. Regular communication through neighborhood associations and printed materials regarding neighborhood activities, accomplishments, and issues also can be helpful to building community. There is obviously also a need for practical caring that can be offered through ministries at neighborhood churches. In the midst of these considerations, neighborhoods should seek to be comfortable communities for newcomers.

Historical Context of the Chestnut Neighborhood

After Reconstruction ended in the South in 1877, many Southern cities, such as Austin, maintained racial segregation in an attempt to preserve the social system of the antebellum period.

The effects of these racial segregation efforts in Austin continue into the twenty-first century, having resulted in deficient social and physical infrastructures for neighborhoods that have been historically inhabited by blacks. The Chestnut community in East Austin ("Chestnut") is one of the neighborhoods that have been stigmatized by segregation and demonstrates its dire consequences.

In 1909, Austin Mayor A. P. Wooldridge said, "For a variety of reasons, East Austin had not got (sic) her share of good things, not because of discrimination, but because it just happened so."[11] Most East Austin residents would have agreed with the first part of that statement but would have disagreed with the second part. Mayor Wooldridge obviously failed to consider the historical record. Allow me to elaborate.

In 1921, a Ku Klux Klan chapter was organized in Austin, and within a year it boasted a membership of 1,500.[12] In November 1921, a Travis County grand jury investigating this Austin racial hate group found that its members or supporters included the county sheriff, one of his deputies, the police commissioner, the chief of police, and one of his detectives—a rather influential group of people.[13]

In 1928, the City of Austin Master Plan ("Plan") was adopted after consultants proposed it as a way to guide anticipated growth. It was designed to regulate race relations in education, entertainment, housing, and most other aspects of social interaction. Indeed, Austin's approach to race relations was commonplace in many cities in the United States, and the structure of racial segregation and discrimination at the turn of the twentieth century was extended by the adoption of Jim Crow-type laws.[14]

The consultants recognized the illegality of racial zoning as a result of the U. S. Supreme Court's decision in Buchanan v. Warley[15], so they designed a strategy to "produce the same result by the selective provision of racially segregated [city] services."[16] Their advice was as follows:

> *There has been considerable talk in Austin, as well as other cities, in regard to the race segregation problem. This problem cannot be solved legally under any zoning law known to us at present. Practically all attempts of such have proven unconstitutional.*
>
> *In our studies in Austin we have found that the Negroes are present in small numbers, in practically all sections of the city, excepting the area just east of East Avenue and south of the City Cemetery. This area seems to be all Negro population. It is our recommendation that the nearest approach to the solution of the race segregation problem will be the recommendation of this district as a Negro district; and that all the facilities and conveniences be provided the Negroes in this district, as an incentive to draw the Negro population to this area. This will eliminate the necessity of duplication of white and black schools, white and black parks, and other duplicate facilities for this area.[17]*

Accordingly, the city of Austin circumvented the illegality of racial zoning by adopting the Plan, which concentrated various services for blacks in "East Austin" (the area east of East Avenue, now U. S. Interstate 35).[18] Such services and restricted housing covenants attracted blacks to the East Austin community and further concentrated them in this area. Notably, Austin's plan was one of five different patterns of residential segregation in cities in the second decade of the twentieth century.[19]

The Plan also designated most of East Austin for industrial zoning and allowed industries to abut residential areas.[20] The city of Austin also excluded the "Negro areas" of East Austin, Clarksville, and Wheatsville from being connected to water and sewage lines, while it extended these public services to the city in general.[21] While East Austin was within the sewer area at the end of 1930, many homes were not connected; and, Clarksville and Wheatsville were still excluded from the system.[22]

> *"The exclusion of Wheatsville and Clarksville from the sewerage system after 1927 was not accidental. It was part of [the Plan] in which public facilities were to be systematically apportioned to black residents of Austin."*[23]

Notably, the only city parks for Mexican Americans and African Americans were located in East Austin. [24]

Segregated housing also encouraged Mexican Americans to live in the East Austin community, although the Plan and segregation laws were enacted before the large increase in Mexican immigration to Austin and Texas in general. Consequently, the laws were applied specifically to blacks and not to Mexican Americans. Nevertheless, Austin was like many Southern cities, in that "[t]he most prevalent and widespread segregation of living areas was accomplished without need for legal sanction. The black ghettos of the 'Darktown' slums in every Southern city were the consequence mainly of the Negro's economic status, his relegation to the lowest rung of the ladder." [25]

By the 1940s, East Austin was a thriving community of homes, churches, small businesses, and professional offices, with 11th and 12th streets as the main business thoroughfares for blacks. Notably, in 1957, the Plan was again accepted by the City Council and reprinted by the Austin Department of Planning as a guide to future development.

Chestnut is a part of the city of Austin's turn-of-the-century urban core and was historically primarily an African American community. It is also one of the East Austin neighborhoods that was affected by the 1928 Plan and therefore affected by racism. It is now a redeveloping residential area bordered on the south by 12th Street, on the north by Martin Luther King, Jr. Boulevard (formerly 19th Street), on the east by Miriam Street, and on the west by Chicon Street. It is about sixty square blocks, or 180 acres. It is less than two miles from U. S. Interstate 35, which is seen as the social class dividing line between racial ethnic groups and the Anglo community. When it is said that someone lives or something is "east of 35," that means that it is located in the African American and Hispanic communities.

Chestnut now has six churches, all of which are black. It is close to downtown and major landmarks such as the Texas State Capitol, the redeveloping site of the former Robert Mueller Airport, the main campus of the University of Texas, Huston-Tillotson University, St. Edward's University, Concordia University, Austin Presbyterian Theological Seminary, Episcopal Seminary of the Southwest, and Austin Graduate School of Theology. Regrettably, none of these seminaries are involved in the East Austin community, but it would be helpful if they were engaged in urban ministry training, particularly for ministers in the Austin area.[26]

Vacant for more than 25 years and formerly occupied by a concrete manufacturing plant, a 22-acre industrial tract is located within the neighborhood. This tract, the largest tract of vacant land in East Austin's inner core, has great potential for revitalization in the Chestnut neighborhood and is now being developed by a local technology philanthropist.

East Austin, including Chestnut, continues to be viewed as the community primarily occupied by African Americans and

Mexican Americans. It is one of the areas most severely affected by several adverse conditions. The area is well above average in characteristics known to contribute to community problems, such as households below the poverty line, adults without high school diplomas, households with single mothers, and unusually high concern about issues such as community problems, family problems, and/or basic necessities such as food, housing, and jobs.[27] It is also an area where a substantial number of the residents, perhaps as many as half, rent rather than own housing.

Without question, the Chestnut neighborhood has experienced racism and socio-political neglect. It has no park, although a small pocket city park was recently built in the neighborhood as a result of recent community transformation efforts. Beyond that, it has no playground or facilities for families or children, other than church grounds and facilities. So the neighborhood youth have been required to play in a park established in 1929 as the "Rosewood Avenue Park and Playground for Colored," located in the Rosewood neighborhood adjacent to Chestnut. The children also have used the fenced-in and unused 22-acre industrial tract as a playground.

Chestnut streets and sidewalks continue to be in need of improvement, although the city government has made some recent investments in these areas. There is, nevertheless, a concern about overall environmental quality and an ongoing need to clean up alleys, streets, and vacant lots. Public safety, health, and youth issues also need to be addressed.

The neighborhood also desires and needs low- and moderate-income residential housing that is available for purchase and is compatible with the original housing style of the neighborhood. Indeed, until recently, Chestnut had about one hundred vacant lots, riddled with tax liens and title problems, on which housing once existed. But the existing housing in Chestnut continues to be an asset. More than one hundred structures within the Chestnut neighborhood are listed in the city's East

Austin Survey of Cultural Resources. Many houses within the neighborhood reflect classic design features. Yet because of their age, approximately 25 percent to 30 percent of these homes are in need of repair or rehabilitation. Notably, some people moving to Austin because of its status as a city of ideas are looking in Chestnut for housing because of its proximity to downtown and the state government complex.

According to the 2000 census, approximately sixteen hundred residents live in Chestnut's estimated five hundred households, as opposed to fourteen hundred residents in the 1990 census. The 2000 census notes that approximately 52 percent of its residents are African-American, 42 percent are Hispanic/Latino, and 5 percent are Anglo, while 14 percent of the residents are senior citizens and 19 percent are between the ages of 5 and 17. By contrast, the 1990 census noted that approximately 77 percent of its residents were African-American, 19 percent were Hispanic/Latino, and 4 percent were Anglo. The 1980 census noted that 88 percent of the Chestnut area residents were African American. Based on current participation in the neighborhood association, it also appears that more Anglo middle-class people are moving into the neighborhood. Accordingly, it is clear that Chestnut is in racial, cultural, and economic transition, and is being gentrified.

East Austin, including Chestnut, is also tainted with the negative perception of being a crime-plagued community. Yet the former Austin police chief stated recently that this community has no greater problem with crime than any other part of the city.[28] Some neighborhood residents suspect the chief's statements were made to support the position that a heightened police presence and investment are not necessary. In any case, the perception has affected the revitalization of the neighborhood, because people believe East Austin has high levels of crime.

While most of the neighborhood residents desire revitalization and many have been expecting East Austin revitalization since the 1980s,[29] they are concerned about the "double-edged sword" effect. In other words, revitalization will result in an improved quality of life for those who live in the neighborhood. Hopefully the neighborhood residents will benefit and the neighborhood's historical values and traditions can be preserved in the midst of these efforts. Simultaneously, however, revitalization will attract higher-income people who desire to live near downtown, the state government buildings, and nearby colleges and universities. These new residents may effectively displace the indigenous residents, who will not be able to afford the prices and property taxes on renovated and new houses. These concerns bring back bitter memories to neighborhood residents of "urban removal" left by urban renewal, a nationwide slum clearance program undertaken in the 1960s and 1970s, which caused many African Americans in Austin and other American cities to be displaced from and lose the homes where they and their parents were born.

Nevertheless, it is clear that East Austin will be the next area of major development in Austin because the city faces an affordable housing crisis and can no longer extend into the western, southern, and northern parts of the city limits with significant housing developments. There are many vacant lots in East Austin that offer great opportunities for in-city residential housing development. The site of the former airport, located in East Austin and about three miles from Chestnut, is also being developed into a major commercial, entertainment, and residential community. Business and commercial development on 11th and 12th streets in East Austin, on the southern boundary of Chestnut, is also underway. Consequently, development is coming to East Austin and to Chestnut in particular. Not surprisingly, Chestnut residents and property owners want to have significant input into its development and want to preserve its African American heritage. Therefore, it is imperative for the Chestnut revitalization initiative to be intentional about preserving and controlling social and physical "space" for the neighborhood. Completing the neighborhood pocket park with plaques or signs that note the neighborhood's history was helpful to preserving social or historical space. Developing neighborhood-owned and controlled affordable housing and rehabilitating existing housing can also provide some personal security or protection for the indigenous low-income residents as the neighborhood becomes economically mixed.

Organized in 1924, the David Chapel Missionary Baptist Church, a black congregation, moved from a blacksmith shop in the Ceiling Hills community to Chestnut and 14th streets in the predominantly African American Chestnut neighborhood in East Austin in 1926. A wood tabernacle was constructed for worship at the new location. It subsequently was torn down and replaced by a stucco building on the same site. Since 1959, the church facilities have been located on Martin Luther King, Jr. Boulevard (formerly 19th Street), a major east-west thoroughfare through East Austin, at Chestnut Street.

David Chapel, the largest congregation in Chestnut and one of the largest black congregations in Austin, has grown to be a predominantly African American, economically diverse congregation of about eight hundred active members representing five generations in some families. Its current primary growth is among people between their mid-20s and early 50s.

Consistent with other black congregations in East Austin, most of David Chapel's members do not reside in the neighborhoods adjacent to its facilities. Likewise, many of the churchgoers in Chestnut are members of congregations outside of the neighborhood. Perhaps this phenomenon has to do with people being willing to drive fairly long distances to attend houses of worship, as well as new housing development being largely outside East Austin. Indeed, there is no longer a community in Austin that is predominantly African American, and African Americans are geographically scattered throughout the Austin area. Yet the African Americans who still travel to worship in East Austin, where most local black churches still are located, are willing to do so to connect culturally and to be involved with congregations that are seeking to make a difference in the community.

Eldin Villafañe makes the following observation about the Hispanic church that can be applied equally to the black church within its own cultural context:

> *The Hispanic church in the barrios has been the locus of cultural validation. Family values, language, music, art, custom, and symbols of Hispanic and Latino pueblo have been sustained, nourished, and affirmed in the Hispanic church. When the dominant culture pressed for a forced assimilation, many found their Hispanic culture and values safeguarded in the enclaves of our Hispanic churches. . . . It is in the many Hispanic churches in our barrios that many find their culture—their lives—affirmed.*[30]

This cultural bond appears to be one reason people are willing to drive to David Chapel from throughout the Austin area and beyond. Consequently, David Chapel has a regional focus and considers itself a church with a heart for the overall community. Notably, I believe that it is not essential for church members to live in a neighborhood in order for a church to be a partner in neighborhood transformation, so long as the congregation acts collaboratively with the affected neighborhood in a significant way.

On June 27, 1997, I learned of a new planning initiative by the city of Austin to encourage self-determined development through neighborhood-wide plans. This initiative would directly affect the residents and property owners in three neighborhoods that were to be selected through the application process. In concept, it was an opportunity for the neighborhoods to take control of their destiny.

The same date I learned about the initiative was the deadline for applications to be submitted. Information had been mailed to neighborhood associations, including the Chestnut Addition Neighborhood Association, which had not expressed interest in the initiative. So by the end of the workday, with the assistance of church members, I submitted an application on behalf of David Chapel to provide leadership for a Chestnut Neighborhood Plan ("Plan"). We submitted the application because of our belief that our Christian faith requires us to be engaged in our community, coupled with our congregation's desire and need to protect the church's interests as the neighborhood underwent redevelopment.

In August 1997, Chestnut was chosen from a pool of fifteen applying neighborhoods as one of the three that would be part of the pilot project,[31] and the city of Austin designated two city departments to assist with the Plan's development. In a sense, it was an experiment.

I subsequently met with the leaders of the Chestnut neighborhood association to explain the program and urge their support and participation in the planning process. Some neighborhood people were skeptical about the project; they seemed to remember the negative effects of urban renewal, which had led to a lack of trust based on previous poor relations with local government. They also wanted to know the motivation for my interest and David Chapel's interest in the project. Nevertheless, I found a nucleus of people who were proud of their neighborhood, and who were interested and committed to being involved in the revitalization efforts. A neighborhood leadership team was selected to guide the process, and I was selected as the chairman. We sought to make the team reflective and representative of the ethnic diversity of the neighborhood. Unfortunately we were not successful in obtaining Hispanic participation on the leadership team. Over the next two years, the leadership team developed the Plan through a community involvement process. We proceeded to secure neighborhood buy-in from the stakeholders, residents, and property owners. The team members, along with city staff, promoted and held neighborhood-wide planning meetings. They conducted three door-to-door surveys in English and Spanish. The also conducted community workshops and comprehensive neighborhood assessments, and they developed a neighborhood communication system. Neighborhood focus groups were held on issues related to housing, community development, public safety, land use, youth development, health, and transportation. All organizing meetings and materials were in English and Spanish. A non-profit corporation to purchase neighborhood property and develop low- and moderate-income housing on it was subsequently incorporated and is presently developing affordable housing in the neighborhood.

The resulting Plan, adopted in 1999 by the Chestnut neighborhood and city of Austin as an amendment to the city of Austin's Comprehensive Plan, covers:

1) land use and transportation,

2) environment and parks,

3) housing,

4) economic development,

5) public safety,

6) youth, and

7) health issues in the Chestnut neighborhood.

The city of Austin has not provided any specific financial or staff assistance to support the Plan's implementation. But in 2001 the Chestnut Neighborhood Revitalization Corporation received an $18,000 grant from the city of Austin for a beautification project and neighborhood newsletter. Now that Chestnut has an approved neighborhood plan, the challenge is the ongoing need to update the Plan and maintain its integrity while it is being implemented. The primary goal is to revitalize the neighborhood through an "asset-based community development" strategy[32] and collaborative partnerships with local governments, businesses, and non-profit organizations. One partner has been the Austin Idea Network, a nonprofit organization made up of people from the creative class, which has joined Chestnut in its revitalization effort. But a challenge to engaging outside partners is that some may become involved in the belief that the neighborhood needs a savior or parent rather than a partner in a relationship of mutual respect.

Chestnut will use the asset-based strategy to focus on the neighborhood's gifts, capacities, and assets rather than on its needs or deficiencies. If Chestnut is to be successfully revitalized, it will need to continue to discover and develop its own capacities without developing dependence on outsiders.

Villafañe has described a typology of social ministry as "helping make the fishing pond."[33] It is an approach to social development that provides a skill and develops resources. There are five principles or tasks to this approach: reviving community life, strengthening local institutions, strengthening support networks, focusing on relationships, and building community assets. This is essentially the approach envisioned in the Plan's revitalization effort. David Chapel's approach to the revitalization initiative is to "help make the fishing pond" in Chestnut. Accordingly, a matrix has been developed to delineate who is responsible for what tasks of the Plan, and this matrix serves as a good management tool to aid the Plan's effective implementation.

David Chapel's role is to partner and collaborate with Chestnut and other entities in revitalizing the area and to participate in its transformation, so that revitalization can be self-sustained. Beyond our having our members participate in the project, making our facilities available for community activities, providing financial support, and being engaged in neighborhood issues, David Chapel desires to be a spiritual resource for the community. Indeed, I agree with Walter Tilleman, who says:

> *I am assuming that the church does have a significant role in the community beyond that of preaching the gospel. The church is more than an encourager of community organizations; the church is more than a source of funds; the church is more than a place for meetings to occur. The church is a catalyst for the spiritual transformation of any community. Church history has clearly demonstrated that assumption whether it be Calvin's Geneva, Chalmers' Glascow, or Edwards' Northhampton.*[34]

C. Eric Lincoln further helps inform one's understanding of David Chapel's role in Chestnut and beyond when he discusses the influence of the black church:

> *To understand the power of the Black Church it must first be understood that there is no disjunction between the Black Church and the Black community. The Church is the spiritual face of the Black community, and whether one is a "church member" or not is beside the point in any assessment of the importance and meaning of the Black Church.... The Black Church, then, is in some sense a "universal church," claiming and representing all Blacks out of a long tradition that looks back to the time when there was only the Black Church to bear witness to "who" or "what" a man was as he stood at*

> *the bar of his community. The Church still accepts*
> *broad-gauge responsibility for the Black community*
> *inside and outside its formal communion.*[35]

In a sense, David Chapel's continuing presence and participation in Chestnut's revitalization says that we believe Chestnut is holy ground, and we will not forfeit God's territory. This is our primary motivation for involvement in the partnership—to be a catalyst for the spiritual and physical transformation of Chestnut and beyond, not only for the black community but for others as well.

In order to facilitate this transformation, David Chapel continues to pray for the community and has strategically planned to develop, over the next five years, its ministries and presence in the community as it strives to be a church that offers hope, healing, and hospitality to its members and others. It will take time and patience. Yet perseverance in such an effort can be aided by understanding that neighborhood revitalization is fundamentally about restoring "prodigal communities" to a state of existence consistent with God's intended purposes. Therefore, it is important that Christians and the church develop and embrace a theology of urban ministry for community revitalization. Having biblical and theological underpinnings for the revitalization effort is crucial for a full understanding of the opportunities, challenges, and goals of the work.

Holy Change

4

Applying a Systemic Tool to Facilitate Community Transformation

*T*his analysis for community transformation takes place within the context of two approaches used in systemic thinking: learning teams and the hexagon technique. Again, a learning team is a team that develops the capacity "to think and act in new synergistic ways, with full coordination and a sense of unity, because team members know each other's hearts and minds ...they develop the capacity to use their disagreements to make their collective understanding richer."[1] "The hexagon technique is an elaborate method of brainstorming. Using this method, we can produce a diagram . . . that describes the cumulative wisdom of a group of people on the topic they discuss."[2] The elements of this technique are:

1. One magnetic whiteboard, about three by four feet.

2. Magnetically-backed, plastic-laminated hexagons, about five or six inches wide, on which are written brief statements that are visible to the group.

3. Dry-erase markers.

4. A facilitator who processes the group's information.

5. A clear statement that can elicit the informed comments of the group.

6. A recording secretary for the group.

This tool was utilized in the Chestnut neighborhood revitalization process, and its use was actually pre-dated by on-going monthly meetings of the Chestnut neighborhood leadership team that were held beginning in 1997. Later, these meetings were held weekly.

This team was established to give leadership to the development and implementation of the transformation efforts for the neighborhood. The leadership team has served as a learning team since its inception.

The team has considered what promotes and prevents transformation of the neighborhood, using the hexagon technique as a methodological tool. It also included a systemic study of the implementation of the transformation partnership in the neighborhood. We also developed strategies to maximize transformation while minimizing hindrances. These intervention approaches should be instructive for other community transformation efforts, whether or not a church is a partner in the effort.

The Systemic Experiment in the Chestnut Neighborhood

The relationship of the Chestnut neighborhood and the David Chapel Missionary Baptist Church is grounded in the Chestnut Neighborhood Plan, which is designed to transform and empower the neighborhood in collaboration with governmental and private entities.

In September 2000, eight members of the Chestnut Neighborhood Plan leadership team held two meetings totaling more than six hours. At these meetings, the hexagon technique was used. The members benefited from previous discussions that had taken place on a regular basis since they had first started meeting in 1997. The results from these two meetings were the outgrowth of much commitment and interaction from the participants. Through my theological and personal reflections, I drew lessons and implications for ministry for other urban congregations and neighborhoods.

The development of the Chestnut Neighborhood Plan identified the real issues that dominate the lives of the people in the Chestnut neighborhood and led to the Chestnut Neighborhood-David Chapel Missionary Baptist Church revitalization partnership. This effort mobilized the Chestnut neighborhood residents to take action together to identify and defeat, in a collaborative and focused way, the social and spiritual forces attacking the neighborhood. A volunteer team of seven neighborhood residents and three David Chapel members, one of whom was a current neighborhood resident and another a former neighborhood resident of more than twenty years, was selected by the neighborhood to give leadership to the Plan's development. I was selected as the team's chairman. The Chestnut Neighborhood Revitalization Corporation, which focuses on the housing development component of the Plan, was also established as a result of the Plan.

Transformation of the Chestnut neighborhood has been greatly facilitated by identifying what factors promote and prevent its revitalization. Developing strategies to maximize revitalization while minimizing hindrances will be of great value to this effort.

Utilizing the hexagon technique allows one to obtain and diagram a wholistic view of the complex system in which the neighborhood transformation effort operates. It identifies the elements of the system that drives and hinders the revitalization effort, as well as intervention strategies that will ensure progress. It enables the leadership team to achieve the goal of long-term transformation.[3]

Using the Hexagon Technique[4]

The Chestnut Plan leadership team served as the learning team in this experiment. The learning team consisted of eight members of the leadership team, including me. Other members were four longtime neighborhood residents. The remaining two members were David Chapel members, one of whom previously lived in the neighborhood for about twenty years and the other one had never lived in the area. The team, therefore, consisted of primarily current and former residents who had historical and recent perspectives of the neighborhood and church.

The members of the leadership team brought a wealth of information and perspective about Chestnut's cultural, racial, religious, and historical contexts. It was commonplace that when the team met, stories, incidents, and observations about the neighborhood were shared that informed the participants of the neighborhood's background. Through this process, the neighborhood's personality and spirit were disclosed. This knowledge greatly assisted this systemic approach to transforming the Chestnut neighborhood.

Two sessions using the hexagon technique were held with the Chestnut Plan learning team. In one session, the team considered what helped transformation of the Chestnut neighborhood, and in the second session, the team considered the hindrances. Each session included grouping the hexagons, on which helps and hindrances were noted, into categories. As participants grouped the hexagons, there was sometimes a need for the proponent of a hexagon to clarify the meaning behind his or her statement. Once the meanings were clarified, participants were able to agree on categories, although adjustments to groupings were not made until final agreement on the categories was reached.

The hexagon group related to the need for sufficient staff, financial support, and other resources had the greatest interrelatedness of the various groupings. It was reinforced, however, by the other groupings, which help transformation of the Chestnut neighborhood.

The initial help[5] and hindrance[6] questions were merged into one question presented to the neighborhood leadership team. It was: "What will help and hinder revitalizing the Chestnut neighborhood?" It was believed that this question would get to the core of the opportunities and challenges in revitalizing the Chestnut neighborhood. The tables and diagrams below record, categorize, and diagram the systemic dynamics involved in the Chestnut Neighborhood–David Chapel Missionary Baptist Church revitalization partnership. They systematically illustrate the responses to that question.

The first table (Table 1) records the actual responses given to the initial "help" question by the hexagon participants. The second set of tables (Table 2) categorizes these responses, which also reflects the work of the team. The third table (Table 3) records the actual responses given to the hindrance question by the hexagon participants. The fourth set of tables (Table 4) categorizes these responses and reflects the work of the team.

The "looping" symbols, called "causal loop diagrams," represent things that reinforce a social reality's direction (i.e., "reinforcing loop") and those things that actually can slow down its direction (i.e., "balancing loop"). The first diagram (Diagram 1) is the initial causal loop diagram for the categories obtained from the initial question. The next diagram (Diagram 2) is the causal loop diagram for the categories obtained from the hindrance question. The last diagram (Diagram 3) combines the two causal loops to make a single causal loop diagram that conveys the story of the Chestnut revitalization system. The areas marked by "L" note the various loops of the single causal loop diagram. "S" shows when the system is moving in the same direction. "O" reflects when the system is moving in an opposite direction. The area marked by "R" is the reinforcing loop of activities that will help revitalize the Chestnut neighborhood. The areas marked by

"B" are balancing loops noting events that can actually reduce the neighborhood's revitalization over time.

Fundamental to the Chestnut transformation story is the observation of Douglas Hall. He notes that we "need to give to God's Spirit all the potentials He has given to us, both our conscious and our intuitive reasoning,"[7] which is discoverable through the application of the hexagon technique to the transformation effort. Seeing what God is using in Chestnut to do His work in the neighborhood and city is crucial.

The single causal loop of Diagram 1 shows that revitalization of the Chestnut neighborhood begins with effective, clear, and consistent communication with all parties affected by the effort. Indeed, this element is the key leverage point because it drives the process toward revitalization. If communication is done ineffectively, it leads to the hindrances in a causal sequence. But if done properly, it leads to sufficient resources to undertake the revitalization effort. The combination of these effective communication and sufficient resources leads to a unified and empowered community. So long as the system operates in this direction, revitalization is under way.

There are, however, opportunities for the Chestnut revitalization initiative to be hindered as seen in Diagram 2. Diagram 3, which diagrams the entire Chestnut revitalization system, notes four balancing loops, which means that there are at least four opportunities for revitalization to be stymied or taken in a different direction. Ineffective communication can hinder revitalization and lead to a lack of committed, informed, trained, and visionary leadership. If there is no intervention at this point, the absence of effective communication will lead to apathy by the community that will result in poor involvement and low participation from the neighborhood. Revitalization will be hindered. Yet, at any point where the system moves in a direction opposite from revitalization, intervention can take place to redirect the process.

Additional analysis and implications of these diagrams will be made in the next chapter. For now, the initial "learnings" contained in these tables and diagrams are self-explanatory within the context of the Chestnut story.

Table 1:
WHAT HELPS REVITALIZING OF
THE CHESTNUT NEIGHBORHOOD?

1.	Communication through newsletter
2.	Volunteers who have time to follow through
3.	Commitment and dedication
4.	Include more neighborhood outreach
5.	Unified neighborhood
6.	Increase youth involvement
7.	More involvement of neighborhood association
8.	Clearer communication among stakeholders
9.	Be consistent
10.	Develop revitalization plan with timelines and benchmarks
11.	Value everyone
12.	Continue involvement of neighborhood residents
13.	Clear, frequent, concise, simple communication
14.	Utilize local and outside expertise
15.	Maintain enthusiasm
16.	Maintain connection with assigned city staff
17.	Neighborhood ownership and development of vacant lots
18.	Recruit volunteers with passion/commitment to neighborhood
19.	Involvement of businesses and organizations
20.	Financial and other support from the city of Austin
21.	Training for neighborhood residents
22.	Set realistic goals
23.	Involve neighborhood residents, property owners, and city of Austin
24.	Need staff for revitalization

Table 2:
WHAT HELPS REVITALIZING OF THE CHESTNUT NEIGHBORHOOD?

A. Effective Communication with Affected Parties
1.   Communication through newsletter
8.   Clearer communication among stakeholders
9.   Be consistent
13. Clear, frequent, concise, simple communication
16. Maintain connection with assigned city staff

B.   Utilizing Sufficient Staff, Financial Support, and Other Resources
10. Develop revitalization plan with timelines and benchmarks
14. Utilize local and outside expertise
20. Financial and other support from the City of Austin
22. Set realistic goals
23. Involve neighborhood residents, property owners, and City of Austin
24. Need staff for revitalization

C. Creation of a Unified and Empowered Community
2. Volunteers who have time to follow through
3. Commitment and dedication
4. Include more neighborhood outreach
5. Unified neighborhood
6. Increase youth involvement
7. More involvement of neighborhood association
11. Value everyone
12. Continue involvement of neighborhood residents
15. Maintain enthusiasm
17. Neighborhood ownership and development of vacant lots
18. Recruit volunteers with passion/commitment to neighborhood
19. Involvement of businesses and organizations
21. Training for neighborhood residents

Table 3:
WHAT HINDERS REVITALIZING OF THE CHESTNUT NEIGHBORHOOD?

1.	Ineffective communication
2.	Negative attitudes
3.	Lack of cleanliness in neighborhood
4.	Breakdown of communication
5.	Lack of workers to perform tasks
6.	Incompletion of assigned tasks
7.	Lack of understanding of tasks
8.	Lack of neighborhood involvement
9.	Inconsistent meetings
10.	Failure to keep our promises or commitments
11.	Insufficient financial support
12.	Non-constructive criticism
13.	Crime in neighborhood
14.	Lack of involvement from businesses
15.	Leader burnout
16.	Failure to achieve
17.	Lack of faith in city government
18.	Lack of safety
19.	Lack of neighborhood priorities
20.	Absence of Spanish interpreter
21.	Not enough vision
22.	Absence of unity regarding vision
23.	Absence of whole community involvement
24.	Lack of code enforcement for neighborhood

25.	Confusing city codes
26.	Failure of city government follow-through on promises
27.	Lack of expediency by community members
28.	Conflicting vision between city government and community
29.	Absenteeism of community leaders
30.	Lack of social activities to celebrate accomplishments
31.	Lack of involvement of Chestnut Addition Neighborhood Association
32.	Lack of leader participation
33.	Residents and property owners will not embrace the vision
34.	Absence of neighborhood historians to tell the story
35.	Identify and develop neighborhood human resources
36.	Lack of opportunity to tell, preserve, and celebrate neighborhood history
37.	Lack of neighborhood political empowerment

Table 4:
WHAT HINDERS REVITALIZING OF
THE CHESTNUT NEIGHBORHOOD?

A. Ineffective Communication Between Affected and Participating Parties
1. Ineffective communication
2. Negative attitudes
4. Breakdown of communication
12. Non-constructive criticism
20. Absence of Spanish interpreter
25. Confusing city codes
34. Absence of neighborhood historians to tell the story
36. Lack of opportunity to tell, preserve, and celebrate neighborhood history

B. Poor Involvement and Low Participation in Our Community
5.   Lack of workers to perform tasks
6.   Incompletion of assigned tasks
8.   Lack of neighborhood involvement
11. Insufficient financial support
14. Lack of involvement from businesses
19. Lack of neighborhood priorities
23. Absence of whole community involvement
26. Failure of city government follow-through on promises
27. Lack of expediency by community members
30. Lack of social activities to celebrate accomplishments
31. Lack of involvement of Chestnut Addition Neighborhood Association
33. Residents and property owners will not embrace the vision

C. Absence of Committed, Informed, Trained, and Visionary Leadership
7.   Lack of understanding of task
9.   Inconsistent meetings
10. Failure to keep our promises or commitments
15. Leader burnout
16. Failure to achieve
21. Not enough vision
22. Absence of unity regarding vision
28. Conflicting vision between city government and community
29. Absenteeism of community leaders
32. Lack of leader participation
35. Identify and develop neighborhood human resources
37. Lack of neighborhood political empowerment

D. Apathy by Community and Public Services
3. Lack of cleanliness in neighborhood
13. Crime in neighborhood
17. Lack of faith in city government
18. Lack of safety
24. Lack of code enforcement for neighborhood

Diagram 1
What Helps Revitalizing of the Chestnut Neighborhood?

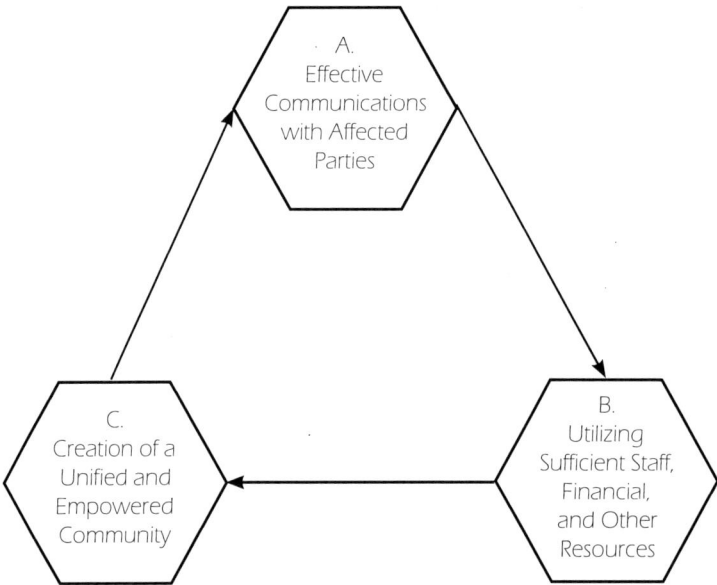

A.
Effective
Communications
with Affected
Parties

C.
Creation of a
Unified and
Empowered
Community

B.
Utilizing
Sufficient Staff,
Financial,
and Other
Resources

Diagram 2
What Hinders Revitalizing of the Chestnut Neighborhood?

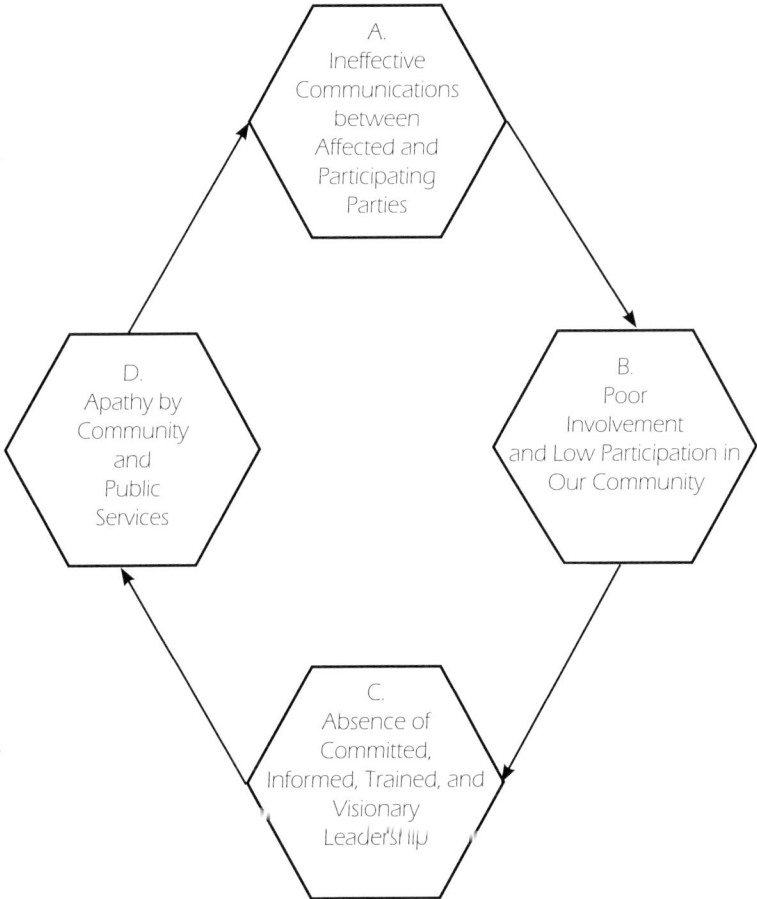

A.
Ineffective
Communications
between
Affected and
Participating
Parties

D.
Apathy by
Community
and
Public
Services

B.
Poor
Involvement
and Low Participation in
Our Community

C.
Absence of
Committed,
Informed, Trained, and
Visionary
Leadership

Diagram 3
The Chestnut Revitalization System

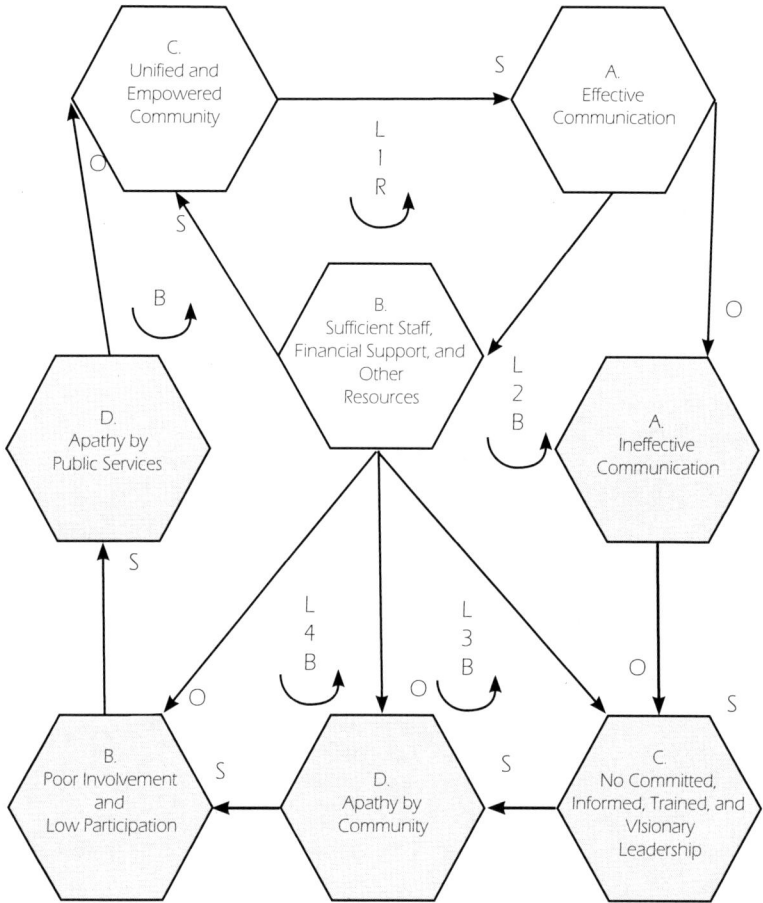

C.
Unified and
Empowered
Community

S

A.
Effective
Communication

L
1
R

O

S

B

B.
Sufficient Staff,
Financial Support, and
Other
Resources

O

D.
Apathy by
Public Services

L
2
B

A.
Ineffective
Communication

O

L
4
B

L
3
B

O

O

S

B.
Poor Involvement
and
Low Participation

S

D.
Apathy by
Community

S

C.
No Committed,
Informed, Trained, and
Visionary
Leadership

S

Some Reflections on the Process

The hexagon exercise assists with discussing shared concerns and hopes, as well as articulating the matters that can help and hinder a neighborhood's transformation beyond the Plan's implementation. This process is beneficial in helping solidify the team's single-mindedness. The hexagoning process also identifies challenges that must be faced in community transformation through a timely implementation strategy. While some in the neighborhood initially questioned the motivation behind David Chapel's application to give leadership to the development of a neighborhood plan, this reaction or roadblock was probably because David Chapel had not previously extended itself to the neighborhood in a substantial way, although a number of neighborhood residents are members of David Chapel. The reaction pointed out the need for improved communication between the church and neighborhood. Perhaps the lack of an authentic relationship between the church and neighborhood, and the fact that most of David Chapel's current members do not live in the neighborhood, led to the initial questioning of David Chapel's motives.

From the very beginning of the Chestnut Neighborhood Plan's development, a conscious and extensive effort was made to obtain the involvement of all neighborhood residents, the two affected neighborhood associations (which later merged), and property owners in the Plan's development process. The city of Austin was also receptive to and supportive of planned development in the Chestnut neighborhood. Approaching the neighborhood with openness and without a specific agenda or any preconceived plan or view of the neighborhood's needs permitted David Chapel to overcome the suspicions about its motivation. Consequently, the neighborhood association, residents, and a significant number of property owners welcomed the opportunity that was presented to them to guide the neighborhood's development and revitalization. They participated in the Plan development process without acrimony, and the neighborhood subsequently approved the collaborative Plan. Therefore, the experience has been a good one and has enhanced David Chapel's relationship with the neighborhood.

Through this process, I learned that urban ministry cannot be done in isolation from other agencies and people in the community. Also, communication is essential to its effectiveness. It is apparent through the hexagoning process that major barriers to revitalization exist. In order to be effective in designing ministry in this context, it is necessary to use effective political skills and influence, have credibility and integrity, be respected in the community and by community and political leaders, and be able to mobilize the community. It is also necessary to be committed to the effort for the long haul. Perhaps more important to designing this ministry is my prayer to see the Lord save and transform people and places, using the church as the base for kingdom agendas.

The city of Austin's pilot project, the beginning of a planning process to encourage citizens to be proactive in determining the future of their neighborhoods, was the impetus for this written plan's development. Designing the project with local government staff assistance was helpful. Although the neighborhood residents and David Chapel were interested in the neighborhood's revitalization, a written plan may not have been viewed by some as the essential primary vehicle for the revitalization strategy. The pilot project, consequently, led to conversations between the church and neighborhood about community interests. If revitalization had been undertaken in the absence of a neighborhood plan, there might have been a greater challenge to developing a common neighborhood vision and a true partnership of mutual respect between David Chapel, the Chestnut neighborhood, and others.

In view of the neighborhood's questions regarding David Chapel's motives, the pilot project gave credibility to the effort. Since the neighborhood did not have a nonprofit organization with staff that could facilitate this process, the initial city and church staffing also assisted with developing the Plan, monitoring its initial progress, and keeping planning efforts on target. Unfortunately, after the Plan was approved by the City Council, much of the staff support ceased and no financial resources have ever been designated for the Plan's implementation, except for a beautification grant that was received by the Chestnut Neighborhood Revitalization Corporation. David Chapel, however, has provided substantial financial and staff support to the revitalization effort.

Not having a plan, however, might have been counterproductive to revitalizing the neighborhood. A neighborhood-approved plan led to a clear statement of the neighborhood's values, interests, and priorities. It was also an incentive in obtaining support from outside partners, such as the Austin Idea Network and technology entrepreneurs, since it removed concerns about internal neighborhood politics and squabbles about the neighborhood's priorities and direction.

It was also helpful to David Chapel to be a part of a collaborative plan as the guide for revitalization. Consequently, David Chapel did not develop its own neighborhood revitalization strategy and arrogantly impose its own vision for what was in the neighborhood's best interest, using its own property and resources, perhaps with government support. The partnership led to shared priorities and values agreed upon by David Chapel and the neighborhood.

Other General Reflections on the Process

The Chestnut neighborhood revitalization process has yielded several results. It has led to a discovery of a new approach to understanding community transformation in general. Such transformation does not take place in isolation. It involves an interdependent and interrelated system. With a common goal and shared vision, transformation requires partners who fulfill their roles and responsibilities while relating to each other with respect.

The residents must take ownership of the process. While there may be many neighborhood residents who initially express interest in the process, it is my experience in this process that there may be only a small nucleus of residents who have the patience, interest, and commitment to be involved in this lengthy and time-consuming process. Consequently, the process must have flexibility to accommodate a changing number of participants while affording all residents at least an opportunity to have input and participate in the process. Without such an opportunity, others may see the transformation vision as belonging only to a small group, and that perception can lead to rejection or resistance in the neighborhood. It has been said, "An internally generated revival can proceed faster and with more lasting effect than if the treatment comes from the outside."[8] Transformation undertaken and owned by neighborhood residents will have a greater impact than if outsiders take the lead.

At its core, effective and sustained community transformation is about understanding the system's operation. One must identify the dynamics in the complex system of community transformation in general and the specific systemic dynamics of the affected community. One must also know and understand how the community's history relates to the city's history. This relationship has certainly affected the community's distinctive personality and collective spirit, and will affect the transformation effort.

One's understanding of the systemic dynamics in community transformation is aided by an awareness of what hinders and helps the process. A fundamental consideration for transformation is the extent of collaboration and communication between the stakeholders. It is also useful to understand that transformation issues are constantly interrelating with each other. For example, the inability of a neighborhood to attract private investments may have something to do with the local government's neglect, poor housing stock, crime, and/or the neighborhood's appearance because of the physical infrastructure or how residents may fail to maintain their property. Therefore, investments or transformation will not be forthcoming if only one issue is addressed. Accordingly, this process affirms the need for a written comprehensive community-specific plan, driven by the community, which addresses the system's dynamics and participants, as the guide for the overall transformation effort.

It is noteworthy that this process has helped me see a neighborhood and its plan as leverage points in developing an overall community. Notably, Douglas and Judy Hall observe: "A movement that is multiplying has the potential to affect entire communities. When vital, relationally-oriented systems grow, they move out from a center in concentric rings like ripples that emanate from the place where a stone enters a quiet pool."[9]

As a historically neglected part of the city of Austin, East Austin is generally in need of more private and public investments. The effectiveness of the revitalization of the Chestnut neighborhood, which is located in the core of the city and a part of East Austin, can have a ripple effect on other parts of East Austin. Although political empowerment will lead to some public investments, the work and investments in the Chestnut neighborhood will produce big returns for East Austin and Austin as a whole over time. Two recent confirmations of this view are:

1) adjacent East Austin neighborhoods, encouraged by the Chestnut planning process, have developed plans to guide their transformation and

2) a Central Texas regional planning process and several adjacent East Austin neighborhood plans, facilitated by the city of Austin, now see the developing 22-acre industrial tract in Chestnut as important to regional and local development.

I, however, have some apprehension about others developing this tract in a way that might conflict with the Chestnut Neighborhood Plan and its priorities, which are so central to the Chestnut revitalization effort.

The process has also led me to have a greater understanding and concern about what it means to build "God's kingdom." I now see neighborhood transformation as kingdom building rather than as simply the social engagement of a church with a neighborhood. Through this process, it has become apparent that there are spiritual dimensions to transformation that may be overlooked if they are not a conscious part of the process, at least by the Christians involved in the process. And a church should always have spiritual considerations in mind. As the good news of Jesus Christ is being offered while a neighborhood is being revitalized and transformed into a place of peace, the kingdom of God is being built.

Therefore, I have changed how I see my city, the neighborhood being transformed, the church I pastor, and my personal ministry. My city and neighborhood are places where I now see an interrelated complex socio-spiritual environment. Efforts to transform the neighborhood must involve not only concerns about physical quality of life issues but also spiritual issues, because the city and the neighborhood are places under spiritual attack. The church must also be sensitive to having a sincere, welcoming, and respectful relationship with its surrounding neighborhood, as well as sincere motivations for being involved in revitalization. The pastor or spiritual leader involved in transformation must take time to engage in spiritual reflection while he or she is involved in the transformation process.

In a conversation with a pastor during the time this process was under way, a striking observation was made to me. He recounted that upon the thirty-year retirement of a pastor of a Houston, Texas, megachurch, the retiring pastor said, "We grew a church, but the city is in worse condition." This statement convicts and urges me to be concerned about the city in which I live and the neighborhood in which the church I pastor is located. No church should be concerned only about building its own kingdom. It must be a catalyst for the spiritual transformation of its community.

5

Applying Systemic Theology to Community Transformation

The Chestnut revitalization project started in 1997, initiated by a church interested in reaching out to the surrounding neighborhood and impacting future development plans that would affect the interests of the neighborhood and church. It led to the Chestnut Neighborhood Plan and its implementation process.

This chapter will consider five principles for community transformation that can be gleaned from the learnings in the previous chapters. Application of these principles to the Chestnut neighborhood project will follow this section. Consideration will then be given to some hindrances, leverage points, and intervention strategies for using a neighborhood plan as an approach to transforming a neighborhood.

Five Principles for Community Transformation

1. Make neighborhood transformation a community priority.

Neighborhood transformation will not be effective or sustained unless it is a community priority. Indeed, neighborhood transformation is fundamentally about building community that goes beyond the physical or social infrastructure of a neighborhood and the resources that may be invested in it.

Community building has been defined as

> *"a focus on the neighborhood as a physical and social whole... comprehensive and coordinated programming to meet human needs...political empowerment or promoting community ownership and governance of change efforts... relationship-building or strengthening the 'social fabric' of a neighborhood."*[1]

I embrace this definition of the community building that must take place within neighborhood transformation.

Christians and the church make no distinction as to secular and spiritual aspects of life because their spirituality is expected to flow through and influence all they do. Accordingly, engagement in neighborhood transformation for the Christian is a spiritual matter. But there may be other people with whom Christians are engaged in neighborhood transformation who may not have the same faith influence. For those who do not share the Christian faith, neighborhood transformation may be seen as simply community work or a secular project devoid of spiritual issues. Irrespective of the motivation for one's involvement in revitalizing the neighborhood, the effort must be a community priority because it is a collaborative process involving the neighborhood—its residents, property owners, and business owners—and its partners. The goal is to implement the neighborhood's vision for its future; therefore, the revitalization effort must a priority of the community.

2. Understand the biblical and spiritual bases of neighborhood transformation.

When a church is involved with a neighborhood transformation effort, as is David Chapel, it is important to understand the biblical basis of the transformation. The example of Nehemiah rebuilding the wall of Jerusalem provides a good basis for such an effort. Nehemiah shows us how people and places, particularly those that have been destroyed, forsaken, and deteriorated, can be transformed with God's help.

Nehemiah's memoirs tell us that his involvement in revitalizing Jerusalem started with his relationships with one of his brothers and others, through whom he learned of the deteriorated and forsaken condition of Jerusalem and its people (Neh. 1:1–4). Because of his relationships with the people and the place, Nehemiah's heart was broken when he learned of what had happened to his community. The first thing he did was pray to God because he believed he must do something for his city. As we begin transforming destroyed, forsaken, and deteriorated neighborhoods, we must also express genuine pain for the condition of those communities.

Nehemiah then began to nurture his relationships with people who could help and support the transformation effort (Neh. 2:4–9). He assessed the condition of the city, developed a plan with the people, and organized them for the work (Neh. 2:11–18; 3). Together they rebuilt the Jerusalem wall, evaluated the process as they built, and overcame the opposition to the rebuilding from within and outside the wall (Neh. 4–6). In transforming a neighborhood, one should expect the same challenges.

Whether or not a church is leading the revitalization effort, many of the findings and principles in this initiative are transferable to any community that desires revitalization or transformation. But resident churches should be involved in the revitalization effort.

It is clear to me that cities are God's prodigal communities, led astray by personal and social sin. They are places of forsakenness and righteousness that struggle to live out God's intended purposes for the city, whether or not the city and its inhabitants are actually aware of these purposes. God desires that all will live peaceably in the city, a safe place that He has established through His grace and mercy. Cities need to be redeemed. As God's representative and agent, the church must actively and strategically engage in reclaiming the city for God's purposes and as holy ground, while recognizing the city as a place of ongoing and active spiritual warfare. Indeed, urbanization of rural communities also makes those areas prodigal communities. Rural churches, therefore, must also see themselves as God's agents and representative in their areas.

One approach to reclaiming the city is for the church to be involved with revitalizing the cities' neighborhoods. In a sense, neighborhood revitalization is about the city or neighborhood coming to itself, much like the prodigal son in Luke 15. But it is not to be an undertaking solely of the church; rather, it must be done in partnership with the affected community.

The church should be a leader in neighborhood revitalization because it adds dimensions to the effort that are absent when others provide leadership. In other words, it should not act as the older brother of Luke 15! A church's leadership speaks to the presence and interest of God in neighborhood revitalization. It suggests that neighborhood revitalization is a "holy undertaking." It also establishes from the beginning that there is a spiritual dimension to what is being done. The participation of the church also offers liberation to the neighborhood and is a catalyst for its spiritual transformation. The church also prays for the neighborhood, which makes a difference in revitalization. It also brings to the process the weight of an institution that is respected in the city, if for no other reason than that it can command the presence of people or church members at public or political forums on community issues. The church must also love and befriend its neighborhood, and demonstrate that love in practical ways. The neighborhood must believe the church considers it valuable. The church must be seen as genuinely interested in the neighborhood. These considerations may be even more important when the majority of church members do not reside in the neighborhood.

The church, therefore, must not pursue its own agenda for the neighborhood separate from the neighborhood's priorities. Neither should it be a "mission on a hill," where it controls enough resources to successfully isolate itself and its ministries from the broader culture around it. In fact, the church cannot minister to a neighborhood in isolation. Nevertheless, the church must be cautious when leading a neighborhood revitalization initiative. Some residents may still see the effort as primarily a church project and may expect the church to carry the bulk of the revitalization load.

In recognizing that neighborhood revitalization is a spiritual matter, it is essential for the church to understand the targeted neighborhood's history and context. A systemic approach to neighborhood revitalization is crucial. From a systemic perspective, it is important to know and identify the neighborhood's culture, history, image, growth dynamics, religious community, heritage, and collective spirit or personality. The "spirit" or "spirits" of the neighborhood and city must be identified.[2]

Of course, what the church does in the community must have a spiritual foundation. There must be a biblical framework for understanding the city and its neighborhoods. The church and its members also must understand its responsibility to the community and what is necessary to do ministry in that setting. In other words, the church must have a "social spirituality that is consistent with the 'following of Jesus.'"[3]

Participating in neighborhood revitalization can also invigorate a church and bring new life. It causes a church to wrestle with its biblical obligations for social engagement. It brings a level of energy to the church and nurtures a servant heart. It leads to care and concern about the surrounding neighborhood. It causes church members to look beyond themselves and feel as if they are making a difference in their community by being salt and light to the world (Matt. 5:13–14). It enhances church members' stewardship. It leads members to stir up their spiritual gifts to the glory of God. It draws others to the church and gives the church an opportunity to share the good news of Jesus Christ. It encourages the church by showing its members that lives can be changed and a neighborhood can be transformed because they, in part, worked to achieve it with God's help.

As the church offers the gift of the good news of Jesus Christ to the neighborhood, it must move deliberately but cautiously in presenting the message. From the neighborhood's perspective, the church must "earn" the right to engage in revitalizing the neighborhood and sharing the message. Through a sincere relationship with the church and practical care from it, the neighborhood residents will be open to spiritual conversations.

3. Identify, nurture, and engage people affected by and interested in the revitalization effort.

Although the revitalization process is for the benefit of the entire neighborhood, the actual workers in the process may be few. But a few committed people can accomplish much. If no active neighborhood organizations exist, it may be necessary for the church or other lead entities to engage in organizing the neighborhood in order to begin the revitalization process. In fact, if there were no formal process to develop a neighborhood plan, such as a city government pilot project, I would start revitalization with organizing the neighborhood, with support from the residents and property owners.

Kenneth L. Luscombe has suggested a useful approach to community organizing that would facilitate this process.[4] He notes that the critical key to the process of organizing a community is the person who does the organizing. He believes this person is "an enabler whose goal is to see people emerge from their powerlessness to self-determination through working together."[5] Once the specific community is selected, the organizer begins to walk among the people, listen to them identify the basic issues of the community, and discover the "community consciousness." This consciousness "forms the invisible symbolic boundaries that mark out more decisively than geography the contours of the community."[6] The people are then brought together to address their issues, determine common goals, form coalitions around these goals, and take small actions that will engender confidence in the people as they achieve their goals. Over time, the organizer brings together the coalitions that lead to a community organization. As the organization develops a common vision and voice, solidarity and support result. This approach would be one way to identify, nurture, and engage the community in the neighborhood's revitalization.

Whether or not there is a formal effort to develop a community organization, neighborhood residents, property owners, and resident business owners are important to the process. I am of the view that these are the people with a direct stake in the neighborhood, so they should develop the neighborhood's revitalization plan, priorities, and strategies so that they can guide their own future. But implementation of the planned neighborhood revitalization should not be limited to residents and property owners. Revitalization is a collaborative effort that involves interested people and entities, irrespective of their location, who can bring relevant resources to the initiative. Accordingly, the implementation of the revitalization strategy should be open to partnerships with interested organizations, businesses, and people who are not residents and have no existing relationship with the neighborhood. Challenges to the ownership and direction of the process are presented when engaging nonresident partners who want to participate in the revitalization effort with goals and approaches inconsistent or in conflict with the neighborhood's priorities. Therefore, the neighborhood initially should determine that these prospective partners have integrity, good intentions, and resources, and can embrace the neighborhood's plan, vision, and approach.

As aspects of the revitalization effort are undertaken, it is important to inform the neighborhood residents of the accomplishments, no matter how small. Although improvements are incremental and often hard-won, communication of these successes is essential. When residents see that revitalization is under way, it will give them a sense of pride and accomplishment and may encourage others to get involved in the process.

Neighborhood residents will also get involved when a sense of community has been developed. One approach to developing this sense is through small, regular interaction and neighborhood-wide special events with neighbors.

It is imperative to identify and develop current adult and younger neighborhood leadership because revitalization is a lengthy process that requires patience. One way to begin this process is to continue to solicit volunteers from the neighborhood association and resident churches. Another approach is to involve youth, from the neighborhood and church, in neighborhood projects, and develop them so that they see themselves as stakeholders in the neighborhood.

It is also important to note that engaging others in neighborhood revitalization has positive and negative effects. The improvement of a neighborhood and the quality of life for its residents also invites others to live in the neighborhood. These newcomers, at least potentially, may not preserve the neighborhood's historical values and traditions. Also, developments such as improved housing and the resulting higher property taxes may lead to physical displacement of low- to moderate-income residents who can no longer afford to live in the neighborhood. A mixed-income neighborhood should be a goal.

4. Embrace the systemic approach to neighborhood revitalization.

Effective neighborhood revitalization is intimately related to partnerships. No one can revitalize a community without collaboration with others because a community is a complex urban setting. No one can fully embrace or understand all the issues that face revitalization without a wholistic approach to addressing a neighborhood's challenges. A neighborhood will not be effectively revitalized without an understanding of a city's systems and the systems' actors, because urban and neighborhood issues take place within an interrelated system. Systems thinking and systemic theology, therefore, are helpful approaches to understanding and developing an effective approach to revitalizing a community.

A systems approach to revitalization helps one understand the urban system in which a neighborhood exists. It also provides a developmental and evaluative framework. But systemic theology allows one to understand and be in touch with God's plan, movement, and redemptive process in the neighborhood's system. Applying the hexagon diagramming process advocated by Douglas and Judy Hall to neighborhood revitalization can facilitate this understanding and one's involvement in the redemptive process.

Revitalization is fundamentally an interrelated, interconnected, and interdependent process involving entities and individuals. Taking a systemic approach allows one to determine what helps and hinders revitalization. One can also discover where to intervene or what to leverage in the system to correct, improve, or sustain revitalization efforts.

If one engages in neighborhood revitalization without understanding the relevant interconnected system, some success may be realized, but it primarily will be through a piecemeal problem-solving approach. If one uses systems thinking in developing and evaluating neighborhood revitalization without the added influence of systemic theology, a system may be understood, but there will be no recognition of how God is working in the system. A systemic approach to neighborhood revitalization is essential.

5. Develop, adopt, and implement a neighborhood-created plan of revitalization.

It is important to believe that most people want to improve their neighborhoods and living conditions, particularly when a neighborhood has lost some of its vitality. Such a neighborhood needs a coherent strategy that can weld together the complex and competing forces that seek to shape it.

I believe that written plans are essential to effective and sustained neighborhood revitalization efforts. A comprehensive, collaborative, community-building, and neighborhood-developed, -adopted, and -driven plan is very useful in developing a common vision or voice, identifying challenges, opportunities and priorities, and adopting certain strategies. It will minimize personal agendas. Since the context of the revitalization effort shapes, promotes, and hinders the revitalization strategies and successes, a plan will necessarily recognize the unique neighborhood context of the revitalization effort.

A plan also will lead the neighborhood to avoid a piecemeal

or disjointed approach to revitalization and will urge the neighborhood to see the future in the midst of the present, which may not be positive. It will also minimize transformation by the "brushfire approach," responding to issues as they surface without much forethought. It also will cause one to see the affected neighborhood within the midst of the whole city. It should recognize the urban system in which the neighborhood must function.

A collaborative plan, properly developed, also will encourage involvement from all neighborhood residents and stakeholders, and will engender credibility in the revitalization effort. Such a plan also will allow prospective nonresident partners to avoid internal neighborhood conflicts as to the neighborhood and priorities. The plan also will cause the neighborhood to identify what personal assets already exist within the neighborhood. In other words, there are some revitalization activities that can be accomplished directly by the residents without outside resources or assistance. Indeed, some aspects of revitalization can occur without financial resources. A plan will help identify these matters.

Consideration of the Chestnut Neighborhood Revitalization System

In order to evaluate the effectiveness of the Chestnut revitalization effort, it is useful to consider its revitalization system within the context of the hexagoning process discussed earlier. In the hexagoning process graphics, symbols are used to diagram a group's intuitive responses in an effort to understand more consciously how a complex social reality operates. The goals of the process are to record and pass on these responses so that "we are better able to make conscious decisions based on what was previously only subconsciously perceived."[7]

The Chestnut revitalization causal loop diagram (Diagram

3) in the previous chapter has one reinforcing loop and four balancing loops. The reinforcing loop (noted on the diagram by "R") indicates what will cause revitalization in the system, while the balancing loops (noted on the diagram by "B") are counterbalancing forces that can hinder revitalization. This means that as revitalization of the Chestnut neighborhood is pursued, there is a high probability that it will be derailed by the noted hindrances that will produce negative results. Key elements in producing effective revitalization include effective communication (particularly of accomplishments), a unified and empowered community, and sufficient staff, financial support, and other resources. However, ineffective communication can lead to apathy by the community and public services, and a lack of committed, informed, trained, and visionary leadership will lead to poor involvement and low participation.

A. Points of Leverage in the System

A leverage is "a change which—with a minimum of effort—would lead to lasting, significant improvement."[8] The Chestnut Neighborhood Plan itself is a strategic leverage point, which indicates the neighborhood's recognition that its revitalization requires an interconnected and planned strategy. But I believe effective communication is the key leverage point because it drives revitalization in the causal loop diagram.

The process also identifies other leverage points that facilitate revitalization. For example:

- Partnerships between the private, public, and religious sectors have been cultivated, nurtured, and sustained throughout the process.

- Opportunities for continuing involvement and collaboration among all stakeholders have been created.

- Timelines and benchmarks for neighborhood revitalization implementation efforts have been developed and monitored.

- A communication system using door hangers, brochures, telephones, and regular reports to the neighborhood association has been developed to inform residents, property owners, and all other stakeholders of the status of revitalization issues and the Neighborhood Plan's implementation.

- Neighborhood volunteers who will be committed to one or more of the revitalization efforts are being recruited continually.

- Relationship-building between the neighborhood and all neighborhood churches continues.

- Efforts are being made to obtain staff to manage the revitalization efforts.

- The priorities of the Chestnut Neighborhood Plan and the overall revitalization efforts are being evaluated regularly.

- The Plan's leadership team continues to meet regularly to monitor revitalization efforts.

- The Chestnut Neighborhood Revitalization Corporation has been organized and is planning to partner with a developer to build affordable housing in the neighborhood.

D. Elements of Counter Productivity in the System

Despite these leverage points, there are some potential hindrances and concerns regarding the points of leverage. Indeed, Douglas Hall has observed that he learned "that what was often counter-productive was what 'I' did to individualistically and directly accomplish something."[9] The same observation can be made when identifying the elements of counter-productivity in the Chestnut revitalization effort. To the extent that the various stakeholders in the Chestnut neighborhood believe they can individually and directly accomplish revitalization without a partnership with one another, there is counter-productivity in the system.

One of the counter-productivity challenges is overlooking the interrelatedness of the residents, property owners, churches, businesses, and governmental stakeholders in the Chestnut neighborhood.[10] For example, it is tempting to look at the issues that affect one or more of the Chestnut churches as being unrelated to issues that affect the overall Chestnut neighborhood. It would be a mistake for residents, property owners, and businesses to believe their issues affect only them. Governmental entities, such as police, health, and public works, also would be mistaken in believing that they could perform their functions alone. In revitalizing the Chestnut neighborhood, it is important for all participants to see the neighborhood as an interdependent system. The revitalization of the Chestnut neighborhood cannot be approached in a dichotomized fashion.

There are other potential hindrances in the system. For example, the inability to recruit and develop neighborhood leaders is a hindrance. Apathy of the community and stakeholders presents a challenge. Government bureaucracy can be a barrier, as well as the unwillingness of public agencies to provide adequate resources and to make implementation a priority. The inability to obtain investments from the private or business sectors may also be a hindrance. Another barrier might be David Chapel's focus on its own survival and ministry interests.

C. David Chapel's Role in the Revitalization System

It can also be said that David Chapel is a leverage point or change agent. Using Jesus' approach in John 10, Douglas and Judy Hall assert that urban people need a "Good Shepherd." [11] They argue the need for true "positive regard" and "relevant communication" from these shepherds. They believe that when city people encounter God's people and see them as people they do not know, "they will have three of the main types of people that deal with sheep in their minds, and they are trying to figure out which one you are."

They ask:

1) Are you a thief or a robber?

2) Are you a hireling?

3) Are you a good shepherd?[12]

The Halls say that when neighborhood residents ask, "Are you a 'thief' or a 'robber'?" they are fearful that you are "coming to check out my place so you can come back later when I'm not here and rip me off; or maybe you're a 'robber' who's gonna pull out a weapon and demand something from me." When they ask, "Are you a 'hireling'?" they suspect "maybe you're a social worker or a preacher who's trying to get me into your church so you can get my offerings. At any rate, you are someone who really cares nothing for me personally but will try to do for me whatever you are paid to do by someone else." When they ask, "Are you a 'good shepherd'?" they want to know whether you are "a person who will ultimately really know, like and care about me for who I really am."[13] As a change agent, it is important that David Chapel be a "good shepherd."

I became David Chapel's senior pastor after serving as an associate pastor for about ten years. After I had spent a few years of preaching and teaching about the church's obligation to reach out to the community and praying for opportunities to do so, God opened a door that allows us to develop the church's heart for holistic ministry to its members and beyond. In 1997, I led David Chapel to apply to give leadership to the Plan, through the city of Austin's pilot project. Consequently, it was important and essential for David Chapel to be intentional and systematic in developing and improving relationships with the residents of the Chestnut neighborhood.

This process has led David Chapel to be a "healing community" where "people with multiple problems and needs are welcome and where they feel they belong."[14] People now find in our church a supportive, therapeutic, and helpful environment through members ministering to one another and others. But as Karen Glasser and Mike Houston state,

> *"The ultimate purpose of a healing community is to be a worshipping body, not a social agency. The healing itself is defined by a Christian understanding, and is inextricably linked to the members' growth in Christian discipleship."*[15]

Accordingly, our vision statement calls us to be

> *"a prayerful, loving and tithing church with a heart for the community that shows its love for Christ by offering God's hospitality, hope and healing to its member and others."*

This is a statement of our vision since I became the pastor in 1992.

Over these fifteen years, David Chapel has realized that it needed to intentionally reach out to its community, both immediate and beyond. This effort resulted in the church embracing a vision that moved it toward eliminating its barriers to community outreach.

In the beginning of this neighborhood-church partnership, there were some people in the neighborhood who tried to identify who David Chapel was and why the church was interested in the neighborhood's revitalization.[16] Although David Chapel had been in the neighborhood since 1926, it never had reached out as it was doing through this effort. Indeed, other neighborhood churches also appear to have had little to no intentional neighborhood outreach in the past. Historically, this lack of community outreach appears to have been the practice of many Austin churches.

Raymond J. Bakke makes an interesting observation:

> *Churches create "climates" and establish cultur-*
> *al boundaries around their churches. The members*
> *of the congregation all wear suits, and the pastor in*
> *the pulpit asks people to come to Christ. What is the*
> *boundary? "You can come to Christ but you must all*
> *dress like us." . . . [T]he pastor is preaching, "Come*
> *to Jesus," but the behavior system of the church is*
> *saying, "We are not of this community. You can*
> *come to Christ if you are of our social class."* [17]

In a sense, David Chapel had created a climate and established cultural boundaries that made the neighborhood residents suspicious when it wanted to do more than have worship and Bible studies, and let outside groups hold meetings in its facilities. Therefore, there were people in the neighborhood who questioned our motives. But the neighborhood started seeing us as a good shepherd as they observed us, heard our heart, and talked and walked with us through the two-year process involved in developing the neighborhood Plan.

As a lead entity, David Chapel will be able to lead and partner with the neighborhood toward revitalization through the Plan to the extent that it is a good shepherd among the people of the Chestnut neighborhood. But there is a risk of the neighborhood becoming dependent on our leadership unless indigenous neighborhood leadership is continually developed. It is also essential to continue to collaborate with the neighborhood and other stakeholders, as well as motivate the leadership team and neighborhood residents to continue to work toward revitalization. David Chapel needs to continue to be "a church with a heart for the community." Also, it needs to be an effective partner with the neighborhood by providing spiritual, financial, and human resources. Revitalization will take place through an effective implementation strategy with sufficient resources.

But the factors that militate against change are the hindrances noted above. Many of them are barriers internal to the neighborhood and its partners. It is essential to be aware of the entire system that is involved with the revitalization effort and develop effective implementation strategies that remove or reduce the hindrances.

An effective partnership between David Chapel and the Chestnut neighborhood will develop and improve as David Chapel continues to demonstrate that it cares about its neighbors and their environment, and understands and will meet at least some of their needs. The desired results will be mutual understanding between David Chapel and the Chestnut neighborhood.

D. Theological Connections to the Chestnut System

Within the context of systemic theology, "doing truth" means not just knowing biblical truth but applying it to real-life situations.[18] As one does truth, "it is important to express a positive concern for the person you want to help."[19] But ultimately, the good news of Jesus Christ is about incarnational outreach, the human touch.[20] Without such an attitude, it will be difficult for David Chapel to have an effective partnership with the Chestnut neighborhood. Indeed, one of my joys of participating in this revitalization partnership is knowing that we have participated in setting processes in motion that will keep on producing long after we are no longer active. [21]

Applying the Principles to the Chestnut Neighborhood

As a church involved in revitalizing a neighborhood, it is essential to begin by stating David Chapel's understanding of revitalization as a community priority and the biblical and spiritual bases of revitalizing the Chestnut neighborhood. It is equally important to consider how the other principles apply to this effort.

1. Making neighborhood revitalization a community priority

I fully recognize that all of the parties involved in revitalizing the Chestnut neighborhood do not have the same faith motivation as does David Chapel. As a church and Christians engage in community work, they must sometimes engage in what others see as simply secular or community work. But whether or not one is motivated by faith, neighborhood revitalization must be a community priority; otherwise, one will not be successful in this collaborative process. The primary way the Chestnut neighborhood determined that revitalization was a community priority was through the Plan that was developed and adopted by the neighborhood. Although this project asserts that a collaborative neighborhood-developed plan is essential for effective neighborhood revitalization, whether or not such a plan is developed, it is crucial that those interested in revitalization determine in some way that the effort is a community priority.

2. Understanding the Biblical and Spiritual Bases of Revitalizing Chestnut

A primary motivator for David Chapel's involvement in the Chestnut revitalization process is its understanding of the spiritual bases for the effort and the responsibilities of Christians to be socially engaged in the community. It is also important to understand that neighborhood revitalization is a spiritual issue in that cities and their neighborhoods have collective spirits that influence their people, institutions, and systems. The collective spirit of Austin is power, politics, ideas, and territorialism. Chestnut's collective spirit can be profiled as an inner-city neighborhood, historically neglected due to institutional racism, which is proud of its African American heritage but cautiously optimistic about its transition into a racially and economically diverse neighborhood. Therefore, as the lead entity in revitalizing the Chestnut neighborhood, this understanding for David Chapel is central to the process.

3. Identifying, Nurturing, and Engaging People Affected by and Interested in Revitalizing Chestnut

As a part of the revitalization process, all neighborhood residents and property owners were identified and invited to participate in the planning process. Although a small number of people have been actively involved in the work, the neighborhood association, as an entity, continues to be a vital participant in the planning and implementation processes. Nevertheless, efforts continue to communicate with and engage other residents and property owners who are not currently involved in the process.

4. Embracing the Systemic Approach to Revitalizing Chestnut

Central to the continuing evaluation of the Chestnut revitalization process is consideration of those matters that help and hinder revitalization, as discovered in the hexagoning process. In the past, it was not uncommon for the Chestnut leadership team to review the hexagoning results periodically to track the progress of the effort, consider the status of the collaborative relationships, and discuss how one aspect of the effort affects another. Using this evaluative tool made it clear that the systemic approach to revitalizing Chestnut had been embraced.

5. Developing, Adopting, and Implementing a Neighborhood Revitalization Plan

This aspect of the Chestnut revitalization process is the most obvious. At the core of the Chestnut revitalization effort is the Chestnut Neighborhood Plan, which casts the neighborhood's vision and priorities. Indeed, the progress that has been made and the ability to engage partners outside the neighborhood have been directly related to the existence of the approved neighborhood Plan. Accordingly, the implementation of the Plan presents the continuing opportunities and challenges.

Revitalizing Neighborhoods and Intervention Strategies

In order to consider the question of how one revitalizes a neighborhood through a neighborhood plan, it is useful to discuss some of the hindrances to such a process. Without beginning with these and considering how to overcome them, it will be difficult to have an effective revitalization process.

Understanding and Addressing Hindrances to Neighborhood Revitalization

Hindrances

Earlier in this chapter, I made reference to some hindrances in the Chestnut revitalization process, which I believe are reflective of hindrances in neighborhood revitalization efforts in general. One hindrance was the extent to which stakeholders in the neighborhood believed they could approach revitalization alone. Another hindrance was overlooking the interrelatedness of the stakeholders. Other barriers identified in the Chestnut revitalization process were the challenge of recruiting and developing leaders from the neighborhood, as well as the apathy of the neighborhood and other stakeholders. The unwillingness of government to provide adequate resources and support implementation, particularly of physical infrastructure issues, was another barrier. To the extent that private investment in the neighborhood is important to its revitalization, the inability to obtain such investments also can hinder the effort.

Similar elements of counter-productivity can be found where urban neighborhood revitalization, like the Chestnut effort, is being undertaken. Attitudes and actions that indicate that the stakeholders

1) do not recognize their issues as also affecting others in the neighborhood, or

2) believe they can address their issues alone will hinder the effort.

Failure to obtain financial, community, and government support may also stifle revitalization. A lack of understanding of the urban system can also hinder effective revitalization.

Some Causes of Hindrances

One of the main causes of hindrances is that some of the stakeholders may be concerned only about their interests and have a higher opinion of themselves than they should. The apostle Paul wrote of this concern in his letter to the church at Philippi (Philippians 2:4). Another cause is that unless people approach a social issue, such as neighborhood revitalization, from a systemic perspective, it is not difficult to miss the interrelatedness of the issues and the affected interests and people. Churches commonly approach involvement in neighborhoods from their own perspectives as to what the neighborhoods need or how the church can benefit. Therefore, they proceed with their own plans. Other causes of hindrance are the attitudes of apathy and resignation of the neighborhood residents, the government, and the business community; they may feel that revitalizing the neighborhood is hopeless. In other words, the cost of their investment in order to revitalize the neighborhood is not worth it.

Suggestions for Removing Hindrances

Churches must begin by developing authentic and caring relationships with the neighborhoods in which they are located. They need to be leaders in revitalizing their neighborhoods. They can begin by allowing their facilities to be used by the neighborhoods for various community-building activities. They also can use their human and financial resources to support neighborhood needs, such as building and rehabilitating houses. But first they must develop a biblical theology of urban ministry that would lead them into this process and may lead them to a systemic understanding. The church must be a healing place for the community so that it will be known that there is a "balm in Gilead" (Jer. 8:18–9:3) that can make the wounded whole.

If local churches are not involved in revitalization efforts, other concerned persons and entities, such as an interested resident or the neighborhood association, can begin with a community–organizing process that will rally the neighborhood residents to express concern about their neighborhood. It could be that having a community meeting will begin the revitalization process and inspire political empowerment that will lead to the involvement of local government.

Leverage Points in Neighborhood Revitalization

In the context of systems thinking, a "leverage point" is "a point at which a small investment of time and resources produces a large return."[22] Accordingly, Douglas Hall states that it is important to identify and nurture these leverage points within a city's complex social system.[23] Among the leverage points in a city are the relationships that exist among the people.[24] Identifying and finding ways to nurture these relationships, particularly among people interested and participating in community transformation, is an effective way to transform a community and permit Christians to fulfill their obligations to participate in redeeming and transforming communities to the glory of God. Therefore, within the context of transforming the Chestnut neighborhood, it is important to identify and nurture leverage points in order to accomplish the neighborhood's transformation.

Some of the key leverage points in revitalizing a neighborhood include identifying the stakeholders and nurturing the interrelatedness of and relationships among them. Indeed, I believe that relationships are vital leverage points in revitalizing any neighborhood. Creating opportunities for collaboration and establishing effective implementation and evaluative strategies will facilitate the process. Effective communication, committed workers, and an effective entity to oversee the effort, such as a non-profit organization, are vital to any neighborhood's revitalization.

Intervention Strategies

Authentic relationships among the people who live in the neighborhood are essential, as are the relationships among stakeholders and others who may be affected by or interested in the neighborhood's revitalization. Beginning with these relationships will lead to other intervention strategies and therefore affect the effectiveness of the revitalization effort. Some of those strategies are enumerated below:

1. If a church in the neighborhood is not involved in the revitalization initiative, efforts should be made to invite and encourage the pastor, church leaders, and/or members to participate in the process because the church brings credibility, visibility, long-term commitment, and pastoral leadership.

2. Where a church is involved, there should be continual teaching and preaching to inform and challenge its members to undertake Christian obligations or responsibilities to be in relationships with one another and their community by having a visible presence in the community and seeking its peace, as representatives of Christ. The interdependence of the congregation and neighborhood can be affirmed. Indeed, an established church may be able to build on its earlier history as it seeks to be involved in neighborhood revitalization. Let God give the church a heart for the community.

3. Where a church is involved, it should equip the members to do ministry in the community and offer ministry opportunities for them to be engaged in such

an effort. Let the church be a place in which people become ministers and receive ministry.

4. Where a church is involved, it can host neighborhood events of food and fun around special days in the year. It can offer job training or employment ministries to the neighborhood, presented by church members or facilitated by established groups. The people may begin to see the church as neighborhood-friendly.

5. Where a church is involved, members and leaders should participate with the neighborhood at events and activities that may occur in the neighborhood. The church should identify neighborhood leaders with whom to begin developing personal relationships and commonalities about neighborhood concerns.

6. Create ongoing opportunities for neighborhood residents and church members to develop relationships among and between each other. It can begin with simple and fun activities that draw the community to a common place where they can greet and meet. It could be something as simple as having a potluck meal and inviting neighborhood residents to bring a favorite dish and games. The church could offer its facilities for one or more of the events.

7. Identify the geographical boundaries of the relevant neighborhood and identify the neighborhood leaders.

8. Convene and conduct a neighborhood meeting to determine and discuss neighborhood concerns. Be aware of language issues. If a neighborhood association does not exist, consider asking about the interest

in organizing one. An association is vital to organizing so that there will be political empowerment.

9. With the support and assistance of neighborhood residents, conduct a door-to-door assessment of the needs of the neighborhood. Be aware of language barriers regarding the assessment's approach. Include an asset assessment that will determine the neighborhood's existing assets, particularly regarding its resources, as well as the skills and talents of the residents.

10. Create opportunities for all neighborhood residents, property owners, and businesses to state their needs; consider a written survey that can be returned to a location in the neighborhood.

11. Using the neighborhood assessment and/or neighborhood meeting, determine the interest of the neighborhood to develop and implement a comprehensive plan that will establish its priorities, guide the revitalization of the neighborhood, identify potential partners who will support the revitalization effort, and assign responsibilities. If the neighborhood chooses to develop a comprehensive plan, ensure a process that gives all affected parties an opportunity for input. Such a process will lead to consideration of the interrelated relationships, interests, and issues.

12. Establish a learning team composed of people interested in and committed to the revitalization process once a neighborhood commitment to develop a neighborhood plan has been made. In this way, there can be ongoing "learnings" as the process continues.

13. Nurture the relationships of the identified potential partners to the revitalization effort.

14. Institute a process to monitor and evaluate the revitalization effort.

ENDNOTES

Introduction

1   Robert C. Linthicum, *City of God, City of Satan* (Grand Rapids, Mich.: Zondervan Publishing House, 1991), 23.

2   Jeremiah 9:11–14.

3   Psalm 46; 48; 122; 147:2; Matthew 23:37–39; Luke 19:41–44; Revelation 21:1–14.

4   Genesis 18:16–19:29; Ezekiel 16:48–50.

5   Jonah 1:1–2; 3:1–4:11; Nahum 1:1–3:19.

6   Jeremiah 29:4–7; 50:1–17; 51:6–10; Daniel 1:1–21; 2:47–49; 3:1–7; Revelation 18:2–10, 24.

7   W. Harold Mare, "1 Corinthians," *The Expositor's Bible Commentary*, gen. ed. Frank E. Gaebelein (Grand Rapids, Mich.: Zondervan Publishing House, 1976), 176; Everett Ferguson, *Backgrounds of Early Christianity*, 2nd edition (Grand Rapids, Mich.: Eerdmans Publishing Co., 1993), 64.

8   Wayne A. Meeks, *The First Urban Christians: The Social World of the Apostle Paul* (New Haven, Conn.: Yale University Press, 1983), 44.

9   Eldin Villafañe, *Seek the Peace of the City* (Grand Rapids, Mich.: Eerdmans Publishing Co., 1995), 22.

10 Meredith G. Kline, *Kingdom Prologue* (Overland Park, Kan.: Two Age Press, 2000), 16.

11 Ibid.

[12] Genesis 4:17.

[13] Ibid.

[14] Eldin Villafañe, class lecture notes, Boston: Gordon-Conwell Theological Seminary, June 5, 2001; Ronald D. Pasquariello, Donald W. Shriver, Jr., and Alan Geyer, *Redeeming the City: Theology, Politics, and Urban Policy* (New York: The Pilgrim Press, 1982), 25.

[15] Genesis 4:20–22.

[16] Psalm 87:1–2.

[17] There was a brief Catholic mission in 1730. Presbyterian and Methodist churches were founded in 1839, and the first Baptist church was founded in 1847.

[18] John P. Kotter and Dan S. Cohen, *The Heart of Change* (City: Publisher, 2002), 1.

[19] Romans 12:1-2

Chapter 1 - A Theology of Urban Ministry for Community Transformation

[1] Raymond J. Bakke, *The Urban Christian: Effective Ministry in Today's Urban World* (Downers Grove, Ill.: InterVarsity Press, 1987), 146.

[2] Ibid., 63.

[3] Ibid., 64.

[4] Raymond J. Bakke, *A Theology as Big as the City* (Downers Grove, Ill.: InterVarsity Press, 1997), 62–64.

[5] Roger S. Greenway and Timothy M. Monsma, *Cities: Missions' New Frontier* (Grand Rapids, Mich.: Baker Books, 1989), 28.

[6] "Systems" includes structures and social institutions.

[7] Tony Campolo, *Revolution and Renewal* (Louisville, Ky.: Westminster John Knox Press, 2000), 247.

[8] Charles Van Engen and Jude Tiersma, eds., *God So Loves the City* (Monrovia, Calif.: MARC, 1994), 30.

[9] Greenway and Monsma, *Cities: Missions' New Frontier*, 28.

[10] Eldin Villafañe, *Seek the Peace of the City* (Grand Rapids, Mich.: Eerdmans Publishing Co., 1995), 19.

[11] Robert C. Linthicum, *City of God, City of Satan* (Grand Rapids, Mich.: Zondervan Publishing House, 1991), 46.

[12] Ibid., 65–66. The same can be said about an urban region as regional planning develops.

13   Emile Durkheim, *The Elementary Forms of the Religious Life*, trans. Joseph W. Swain (New York: Free Press, 1915), 29.

14   Albert H. van den Heuvel, *The Rebellious Powers* (New York: Friendship Press, 1965), 58.

15   Ibid., 42.

16   Jayakumar Christian, *God of the Empty-Handed* (Monrovia, Calif.: MARC, 1999), 150.

17   Linthicum, *City of God, City of Satan*, 68–73; van den Heuvel, The Rebellious Powers, 58.

18   Villafañe, *Seek the Peace of the City*, 20.

19   "Apostle To The City" (Interview by Richard A. Kariffman), *Christianity Today*, March 3, 1997, 37-40; Bakke, *A Theology as Big as the City*, 62.

20   Ronald D. Pasquariello, Donald W. Shriver, Jr., and Alan Geyer, *Redeeming the City: Theology, Politics, and Urban Policy* (New York: The Pilgrim Press, 1982), 17.

21   Bakke, *A Theology as Big as the City*, 62.

22   Linthicum, *City of God, City of Satan*, 41–47.

23   Ibid., 105.

24   Villafañe, *Seek the Peace of the City*, 19.

25   H. Richard Niebuhr, *Christ and Culture* (New York: Harper & Row, 1951), 223–225.

26   Villafañe, *Seek the Peace of the City*, 20.

27   Niebuhr, *Christ and Culture*, 43.

28   Pasquariello, Shriver, and Geyer, *Redeeming the City: Theology, Politics & Urban Policy*, 7.

29 Ibid.

30 Ronald J. Sider, *Cup of Water, Bread of Life* (Grand Rapids, Mich.: Zondervan Publishing House, 1994), 165.

31 Ibid., 43.

32 Orlando E. Costas, *Christ Outside the Gate: Mission Beyond Christendom* (Maryknoll, N.Y.: Orbis Books, 1982), 14.

33 Ibid., 16.

34 It includes kenosis (vv. 6–7a), servanthood (v. 7a), contextualization (vv. 7b–8a), humility (v. 8), obedience (v. 8b), sacrificial service (vv. 8b, 5–11, 17–30), and redemption (vv. 9–11). Villafañe, class lecture notes, June 5, 2001.

35 Linthicum, *City of God, City of Satan*, 87.

36 See Douglas and Judy Hall, *A Culture of Hope* (Boston: Emmanuel Gospel Center, 2000), 45–47.

37 George G. Hunter, III, *The Contagious Congregation: Frontiers in Evangelism and Church Growth* (Nashville, Tenn.: Abingdon Press, 1979), 20.

38 Greenway and Monsma, *Cities: Missions' New Frontier*, 52.

39 Villafañe, class lecture notes, June 5, 2001.

40 William Fay and Ralph Hodge, *Share Jesus Without Fear* (Nashville, TN: LifeWay Press, 1997), 7.

41 Philip Yancey, *What's So Amazing About Grace?* (Grand Rapids, Mich.: Zondervan Publishing House, 1997), 13–15, 36.

42 Ibid., 16.

43 Ibid., 30.

44 Greg Reed, *Economic Empowerment through the Church* (Grand Rapids, Mich.: Zondervan Publishing House, 1994), 13.

45 Villafañe, *Seek the Peace of the City*, 18.

46 C. Norman Kraus, *The Community of the Spirit* (Scottdale, Penn.: Herald Press, 1993), 136.

47 Howard Thurman, *Jesus and the Disinherited* (Nashville, Tenn.: Abingdon Press, 1949), 13.

48 Villafañe, Seek the Peace of the City, 39.

49 Ibid.

50 Ibid., 37.

51 Ibid., 38.

52 John Perkins and Jo Kadlacek, *Resurrecting Hope* (Ventura, Calif.: Regal Books, 1995), 20.

53 Sidney H. Rooy, "Theological Education for Urban Mission," *Discipling the City* (Grand Rapids, Mich.: Baker Books, 1992), 233.

54 Villafañe, class lecture notes, June 5, 2001.

55 Villafañe, *Seek the Peace of the City*, 36.

56 Christian, God of the Empty-Handed, 33.

57 Villafañe, class lecture notes, June 5, 2001. Acts 6:1–7 (Give a Fish–charity, benevolence), Exodus 35:30–34 (Teach How to Fish–self-help, training, skills), Nehemiah 2:17–18 (Help Make the Fishing Rod–community development, economic development), Proverbs

31:8–9; Acts 16:35–40 (Own/Get a Piece of the Lake–advocacy, congregational-based community organizing, community-conflict transformation).

[58] Tom Skinner, "The Church in the Community," *Biblical Strategies for a Community in Crisis: What African Americans Can Do* (Chicago: Urban Ministries, 1992), 165.

[59] Roger S. Greenway, "Confronting Urban Contexts with the Gospel," *Discipling the City*, 43.

[60] James L. Christensen, *Don't Waste Your Time in Worship* (Old Tappan, N.J.: Fleming H. Revell, 1978), 125.

[61] Craig W. Ellison, "Counseling and Discipleship for the City," *Discipling the City*, 99.

[62] Raymond J. Bakke, "Profiles of Effective Urban Pastors," *Discipling the City*, 134.

[63] Eldin Villafañe, *A Prayer for the City* (Austin, Texas: AETH, 2001), xix.

[64] Clinton E. Arnold, *Powers of Darkness* (Downers Grove, Ill.: InterVarsity Press, 1992), 158.

[65] Kenneth Leech, *True Prayer* (New York: Harper & Row, 1980), 68.

[66] Karen E. Lange, "Djenne–Eternal City of West Africa," *National Geographic* (June 2001), 100.

Chapter 2 - Approaches to Community Transformation

[1]   Douglas and Judy Hall, *A Culture of Hope* (Boston: Emmanuel Gospel Center, 2000), 1.

[2]   Peter M. Senge, *The Fifth Discipline: The Art & Practice of the Learning Organization* (New York: Currency Doubleday, 1990), 7.

[3]   Peter M. Senge, et al., "Strategies for Systems Thinking," *The Fifth Discipline Fieldbook* (New York: Doubleday, 1994), 87.

[4]   Senge, *The Fifth Discipline*, 7.

[5]   Senge, et al, *The Fifth Discipline Fieldbook*, 195.

[6]   Ibid., 235.

[7]   Senge, *The Fifth Discipline*, 9.

[8]   Senge, et al, *The Fifth Discipline Fieldbook*, 352.

[9]   Douglas and Judy Hall, *A Culture of Hope*, 15.

[10]   Douglas Hall, "Systems Thinking and the Urban Church," A-8.

[11]   Ibid., A-12.

[12]   H. Richard Niebuhr, *Christ and Culture* (New York: Harper & Row, 1951), 2.

[13]   Ibid., 32.

[14]   Ibid., 45.

[15]   Ibid., 40.

[16]   Ibid., 52.

[17]   Ibid., 66.

[18] Paul Lehmann, *Ethics in a Christian Context* (New York: Harper & Row, 1963), 112, 174.

[19] Niebuhr, *Christ and Culture*, 83.

[20] Ibid., 41.

[21] Ibid., 103.

[22] Ibid., 120.

[23] Ibid., 123.

[24] Ibid.

[25] Ibid., 150.

[26] Ibid., 42.

[27] Ibid., 167.

[28] Ibid., 190.

[29] Charles Scriven, *The Transformation of Culture* (Scottdale, Pa.: Herald Press, 1988), 20.

[30] Eldin Villafañe, *Seek the Peace of the City* (Grand Rapids, Mich.: Eerdmans Publishing Co., 1995), 1-3; 12-28.

[31] Ibid., 14.

[32] Clifford J. Green, ed., *Churches, Cities, and Human Community: Urban Ministry in the United States 1945-1985* (Grand Rapids, Mich.: William B. Eerdmans, 1996).

[33] Ibid., 83.

[34] Ibid., 247.

[35] G. Willis Bennett, *Guidelines for Effective Urban Church Ministry* (Nashville, Tenn.: Broadman Press, 1983), 22-24.

Chapter 3 - A Systemic Experiment: Transforming the Chestnut Neighborhood in Austin, Texas

1   D. W. C. Baker, *A Texas Scrapbook* (New York: A. S. Barnes and Company, 1875), 142–143.

2   Richard Florida, *The Rise of the Creative Class* (New York: Basic Books, 2002).

3   Mark Lisheron and Bill Bishop, "Why the Creative Class Come Here," *Austin American Statesman* (May 12, 2002).

4   Ibid.

5   Mark Lisheron and Bill Bishop, "Austin's Fast-Growing Immigrant Community Is Source of Wealth," *Austin American Statesman* (June 9, 2002).

6   Ibid.

7   "A Look at the Creative Class," *Austin American Statesman* (April 28, 2002).

8   Ibid.; Mark Lisheron and Bill Bishop, "Austin Boom In '90s Part of Creative Shift in U.S.," *Austin American Statesman* (August 4, 2002).

9   "A Look at the Creative Class," *Austin American Statesman* (April 28, 2002).

10   Mark Lisheron and Bill Bishop, "A Spiritual Awakening," *Austin American Statesman* (December 29, 2002).

11   "East Austin Improvement Club Notes," *The Austin Daily Statesman* (November 11, 1909), 2.

12   David C. Humphrey, *Austin: An Illustrated History* (Austin: Windsor Publications, 1985), 174.

[13] Steven J. Kraus, Water, *Sewers and Streets: The Acquisition of Public Utilities in Austin, Texas 1875-1930*. Thesis, University of Texas at Austin (1973), 147.

[14] C. Vann Woodward, *The Strange Career of Jim Crow, 3rd edition* (New York: Oxford University Press, 1974), 97–117.

[15] 245 U. S. 60 (1917).

[16] Austin Human Relations Commission, *Housing Patterns Study of Austin*, Texas (Austin, Texas: May 1979), 179.

[17] Koch and Fowler Consulting Engineers, Inc., *A City Plan for Austin, Texas* (Dallas, 1928), 71.

[18] Joe R. Feagin and Robena Jackson, "Delivery of Services to Black East Austin and Other Black Communities: A Socio-Historical Analysis" (Final Report on Hogg Foundation, 1985), 33.

[19] Woodward, *The Strange Career of Jim Crow*, 100.

[20] Feagin and Jackson, 34.

[21] Kraus, *Water, Sewers and Streets*, 138–155.

[22] Ibid., 150.

[23] Ibid.

[24] Ibid., 150–154.

[25] Woodward, *The Strange Career of Jim Crow*, 101.

[26] See Eldin Villafañe, Bruce W. Jackson, Robert A. Evans, Alice Frazer Evans, *Transforming the City: Reframing Education for Urban Ministry.*

[27] *First View 2002 for Urban Ministry*(The Percept Group, Inc., January 10, 2002).

28 Stated in a public meeting on July 10, 2002, at David
    Chapel Missionary Baptist Church.

29 James Pinkerton, "East Austin weighs changes," *Austin
    American-Statesman* (October 10, 1984), 1.

30 Eldin Villafañe, *Seek the Peace of the City: Reflections on
    Urban Ministry* (Grand Rapids, Mich.: Eerdmans Pub-
    lishing Co., 1995), 34–35.

31 The other two pilot neighborhoods were East César
    Chávez, a predominantly Hispanic/Latino (83 percent)
    neighborhood in East Austin, and Dawson, an ethnically
    mixed neighborhood (57 percent Hispanic, 39 percent
    Anglo, 2 percent African American, 2 percent Asian
    American) in the south-central part of Austin's urban
    core.

32 This approach to neighborhood revitalization is defined
    as "the development of policies and activities based on
    the capacities, skills and assets of lower income people
    and their neighborhoods." John P. Kretzmann and John
    L. McKnight, *Building Communities from the Inside Out:
    A Path Toward Finding and Mobilizing a Community's As-
    sets*, (Chicago, Ill.: ACTA Publications, 1993), 5.

33 A typology of social ministry taught by Eldin Villafañe
    (June 6, 2001, D. Min. lecture at Gordon-Conwell Theo-
    logical Seminary, Boston, Mass.).

34 Walter Robert Tilleman, "The Role of the Church in the
    Community" (D.Min. project, Gordon-Conwell Theo-
    logical Seminary, 1998), 42.

35 C. Eric Lincoln, *The Black Church Since Frazier* (New
    York: Schocken Books, 1974). 116, 124.

Chapter 4 - Applying a Systemic Tool to Facilitate Community Transformation

1   Eldin Villafañe, Doctor of Ministry residency lecture in the course "The Church in the City: Confronting Issues in Contemporary Urban Society," Gordon-Conwell Theological Seminary, Boston, June 2002

2   Senge, et al, *The Fifth Discipline Fieldbook*, 352.

3   Douglas Hall and Steve Darnan, "Systems Thinking and the Urban Church," *Christianity in Boston: A Series of Monographs & Case Studies on the Vitality of the Church in Boston*, ed. Douglas Hall, Rudy Mitchell, and Jeff Bass (Boston: Emmanuel Gospel Center, 1993), A-10.

4   I also found this technique helpful in facilitating the development of my congregation's strategic plan, and what helps and hinders the congregation's strategic vision.

5   What helps revitalizing of the Chestnut neighborhood?

6   What hinders revitalizing of the Chestnut neighborhood?

7   Hall, Mitchell and Bass, A–12.

8   Jay W. Forrester, *Urban Dynamics* (Cambridge, Mass.: MIT Press, 1969), 6.

9   Douglas and Judy Hall, *A Culture of Hope* (Boston: Emmanuel Gospel Center, 2000), 53

Chapter 5 - Applying Systemic Theology to Community Transformation

[1] Xavier de Souza Briggs and Elizabeth J. Mueller, *From Neighborhood to Community: Evidence on the Social Effects of Community Development* (New York: Community Development Research Center, New School for Social Research, 1997), 173.

[2] See Chapter 1 and under No. 2 principle applied to Chestnut identification of the spirits of Austin and the Chestnut neighborhood.

[3] Eldin Villafañe, *Seek the Peace of the City* (Grand Rapids, Mich.: Eerdmans Publishing Co., 1995), 13.

[4] Kenneth L. Luscombe, "Organizing for Community," *Signs of Hope in the City* (Monrovia, Calif.: MARC, 1995), 56–63.

[5] Ibid., 58.

[6] Ibid., 59.

[7] Douglas Hall and Steve Darnan, "Systems Thinking and the Urban Church," *Christianity in Boston*, A-12.

[8] Peter M. Senge, *The Fifth Discipline: The Art & Practice of the Learning Organization* (New York: Currency Doubleday, 1990), 64.

[9] Douglas and Judy Hall, *A Culture of Hope* (Boston: Emmanuel Gospel Center, 2000), 4.

[10] One could argue that a stakeholder is anyone in the city who is concerned about and committed to all areas of the city being vibrant and "vitalized," so long as the neighborhood vision and plan controls.

11 Douglas and Judy Hall, *A Culture of Hope*, 45–47.

12 Ibid.

13 Ibid.

14 Karen Glasser and Mike Houston, "The Church as a Healing Community," *Christianity in Boston: A Series of Monographs & Case Studies on the Vitality of the Church in Boston*, ed. Douglas Hall, Rudy Mitchell, and Jeff Bass (Boston: Emmanuel Gospel Center, 1993), E-2.

15 Ibid.

16 It appeared as if they were trying to determine whether David Chapel was a "thief" or "robber," a "hireling," or a "good shepherd," terms used by Douglas and Judy Hall in *A Culture of Hope*, 45–47.

17 Raymond J. Bakke, *The Urban Christian: Effective Ministry in Today's Urban World*, (Downers Grove, Ill.: InterVarsity Press, 1987), 57.

18 Douglas and Judy Hall, *A Culture of Hope*, 133.

19 Ibid., 135.

20 Soong-Chan Rah, "Navigating Cultural Currents," *Leadership* (Fall 2000), 42.

21 See Douglas and Judy Hall, *A Culture of Hope*, 137–138.

22 Douglas Hall, "City Growth Missions," *Christianity in Boston: A Series of Monographs & Case Studies on the Vitality of the Church in Boston*, ed. Douglas Hall, Rudy Mitchell, and Jeff Bass (Boston: Emmanuel Gospel Center, 1993), G-2.

23 Ibid.

24   Ibid., G-3. Hall points to the parenting situation as an example of relationships as leverage points.

BIBLIOGRAPHY

Arnold, Clinton E. *Powers of Darkness.* Downers Grove, Ill.: InterVarsity Press, 1992.

Austin Human Relations Commission. *Housing Patterns Study of Austin*, Texas. Austin, Texas, May 1979.

Austin American Statesman. November 11, 1909.

Austin American Statesman. "A Look at the Creative Class." April 28, 2002.

Bakke, Raymond J. "Profiles of Effective Urban Pastors." *Discipling the City.* Grand Rapids, Mich.: Baker Books, 1992.

_____. "Apostle To The City" (Interview by Richard A. Kariffman), *Christianity Today*, March 3, 1997.

_____. *The Urban Christian: Effective Ministry in Today's Urban World.* Downers Grove, Ill.: InterVarsity Press, 1987.

_____. *A Theology as Big as the City.* Downers Grove, Ill.: InterVarsity Press, 1997.

Baker, D. W. C. *A Texas Scrapbook.* New York: A. S. Barnes and Company, 1875.

Campolo, Tony. *Revolution and Renewal.* Louisville, Ky.: Westminster John Knox Press, 2000.

Christensen, James L. *Don't Waste Your Time In Worship.* Old Tappan, N.J.: Fleming H. Revell, 1978.

Christian, Jayakumar. *God of the Empty-Handed.* Monrovia, Calif.: MARC, 1999.

Costas, Orlando E. *Christ Outside the Gate: Mission Beyond Christendom.* Maryknoll, N.Y.: Orbis Books, 1982.

De Souza Briggs, Xavier and Elizabeth J. Mueller. *From Neighborhood to Community: Evidence on the Social Effects of Community Development.* New York: Community Development Research Center, New School for Social Research, 1997.

Durkheim, Emile. *The Elementary Forms of the Religious Life.* Trans. Joseph W. Swain. New York: Free Press, 1915.

Ellison, Craig W. "Counseling and Discipleship for the City." *Discipling the City.* Grand Rapids, Mich.: Baker Books, 1992.

Feagin, Joe R. and Robena Jackson. "Delivery of Services to Black East Austin and Other Black Communities: A Socio-Historical Analysis." Final Report on Hogg Foundation, 1985.

Ferguson, Everett. *Backgrounds of Early Christianity,* 2nd edition. Grand Rapids, Mich.: Eerdmans Publishing Co., 1993.

First View 2002. The Percept Group, Inc., January 10, 2002.

Florida, Richard. *The Rise of the Creative Class.* New York: Basic Books, 2002.

Forrester, Jay W. *Urban Dynamics.* Cambridge, Mass.: MIT Press, 1969.

Frazier, E. Franklin. *The Negro Church in America.* C. Eric. Lincoln. The Black Church Since Frazier. New York: Schocken Books, 1974.

Greenway, Roger S. "Confronting Urban Contexts with the Gospel." *Discipling the City*. Grand Rapids, Mich.: Baker Books, 1992.

Greenway, Roger S. and Timothy M. Monsma. *Cities: Missions' New Frontier*. Grand Rapids, Mich.: Baker Books, 1989.

Hall, Douglas and Judy Hall. *A Culture of Hope* (draft photocopy). Boston: Emmanuel Gospel Center, 2000.

Hall, Douglas. "City Growth Missions." *Christianity in Boston: A Series of Monographs & Case Studies on the Vitality of the Church in Boston*. Ed. Douglas Hall, Rudy Mitchell and Jeff Bass. Boston: Emmanuel Gospel Center, 1993.

Hall, Douglas and Steve Darnan. "Systems Thinking and the Urban Church." *Christianity in Boston: A Series of Monographs & Case Studies on the Vitality of the Church in Boston*. Ed. Douglas Hall, Rudy Mitchell, and Jeff Bass. Boston: Emmanuel Gospel Center, 1993.

Humphrey, David C. *Austin: An Illustrated History*. Austin: Windsor Publications, 1985.

Hunter, George G., III. *The Contagious Congregation: Frontiers in Evangelism and Church Growth*. Nashville, Tenn.: Abingdon Press, 1979.

Kline, Meredith G. *Kingdom Prologue*. Overland Park, Kan.: Two Age Press, 2000.

Koch and Fowler Consulting Engineers, Inc. *A City Plan For Austin*, Texas. Dallas, 1928.

Kraus, C. Norman. *The Community of the Spirit*. Scottdale, Pa.: Herald Press, 1993.

Kraus, Steven J. *Water, Sewers and Streets: The Acquisition of Public Utilities in Austin, Texas 1875–1930.* Thesis, University of Texas at Austin. 1973.

Kretzmann, John P. and John L. McKnight. *Building Communities from the Inside Out: A Path Toward Finding and Mobilizing a Community's Assets.* Evanston, Ill.: Center for Urban Affairs and Policy Research Neighborhood Innovations Network, 1993.

Lange, Karen E. "Djenne—Eternal City of West Africa." *National Geographic.* June 2001.

Leech, Kenneth. *True Prayer.* New York: Harper & Row, 1980.

Lehmann, Paul. *Ethics in a Christian Context.* New York: Harper & Row, 1963.

Lincoln, C. Eric and Lawrence H. Mamiya. *The Black Church in the African American Experience.* Durham, N.C.: Duke University Press, 1990.

Linthicum, Robert C. *City of God, City of Satan.* Grand Rapids, Mich.: Zondervan Publishing House, 1991.

Lisheron, Mark and Bill Bishop. "Why the Creative Class Come Here." *Austin American Statesman.* May 12, 2002.

_____. "Austin Boom In '90s Part of Creative Shift In U. S." *Austin American Statesman.* August 4, 2002.

_____. "A Spiritual Awakening." *Austin American Statesman.* December 29, 2002.

Luscombe, Kenneth L. "Organizing for Community." *Signs of Hope in the City.* Monrovia, Calif.: MARC, 1995.

Mare, W. Harold. "1 Corinthians." *The Expositor's Bible Commentary.* Gen. Ed. Frank E. Gaebelein. Grand Rapids, Mich.: Zondervan Publishing House, 1976.

Meeks, Wayne A. *The First Urban Christians: The Social World of the Apostle Paul.* New Haven, Conn.: Yale University Press, 1983.

Mott, Stephen Charles. *Biblical Ethics and Social Change.* New York: Oxford University Press, 1982.

Niebuhr, H. Richard. *Christ and Culture.* New York: Harper & Row, 1951.

Pasquariello, Ronald D., Donald W. Shriver, Jr., and Alan Geyer. *Redeeming the City: Theology, Politics, and Urban Policy.* New York: The Pilgrim Press, 1982.

Perkins, John and Jo Kadlecek. *Resurrecting Hope.* Ventura, Calif.: Regal Books, 1995.

Pinkerton, James. "East Austin weighs changes." *Austin American-Statesman.* October 10, 1984.

Rah, Soong-Chan. "Navigating Cultural Currents." *Leadership.* Fall 2000.

Reed, Greg. *Economic Empowerment through the Church.* Grand Rapids, Mich.: Zondervan Publishing House, 1994.

Rooy, Sidney H. "Theological Education for Urban Mission." *Discipling the City.* Grand Rapids, Mich.: Baker Books, 1992.

Scriven, Charles. *The Transformation of Culture.* (Scottdale, Pa.: Herald Press, 1988.

Senge, Peter M. *The Fifth Discipline: The Art & Practice of the Learning Organization.* New York: Currency Doubleday, 1990.

Senge, Peter M., et al. *The Fifth Discipline Fieldbook.* New York: Currency Doubleday, 1994.

Share Jesus Without Fear. LifeWay Press, 1997.

Sider, Ronald J. *Cup of Water, Bread of Life.* Grand Rapids, Mich.: Zondervan Publishing House, 1994.

Skinner, Tom. "The Church In The Community." *Biblical Strategies for a Community In Crisis: What African Americans Can Do.* Chicago: Urban Ministries, 1992.

Thurman, Howard. *Jesus and the Disinherited.* Nashville, Tenn.: Abingdon Press, 1949.

Tilleman, Walter Robert. "The Role of the Church in the Community." Doctor of Ministry project. Gordon-Conwell Theological Seminary. Boston. 1998.

Van den Heuvel, Albert H. *The Rebellious Powers.* New York: Friendship Press, 1965.

Van Engen, Charles and Jude Tiersma, ed. *God So Loves the City.* Monrovia, Calif.: MARC, 1994.

Villafañe, Eldin. *A Prayer for the City.* Austin, Texas: AETH, 2001.

_____. *Seek the Peace of the City: Reflections on Urban Ministry.* Grand Rapids, Mich.: Eerdmans Publishing Co., 1995.

_____. "The Church in the City: Confronting Issues in Contemporary Urban Society." Doctor of Ministry lecture handout for the course The Church in the City: Confronting Issues in Contemporary Urban Society. Gordon-Conwell Theological Seminary Boston. June 2002.

_____. "Typology of Social Ministry." Doctor of Ministry lecture handout for the course Seek the Peace of the City: Theology and Ethics for Urban Ministry. Gordon-Conwell Theological Seminary. Boston. June 2001.

Villafañe, Eldin, Bruce W. Jackson, Robert A. Evans, Alice Frazer Evans. *Transforming the City: Reframing Education for Urban Ministry.* Grand Rapids, Mich.: Eerdmans Publishing Company, 2002.

Woodard, C. Vann. *The Strange Career of Jim Crow*, 3rd edition. New York: Oxford University Press, 1974.

Yancey, Philip. What's So Amazing About Grace? (Grand Rapids, MI: Zondervan Publishing House, 1997).

About the Author

Dr. Joseph C. Parker, Jr., a native of Birmingham, Alabama, is a longtime community transformer who has given leadership to the Chestnut Neighborhood Revitalization Initiative in Austin, Texas, among other community development initiatives. He has served as the Senior Pastor of the David Chapel Missionary Baptist Church in Austin, Texas, "a church with a heart for the community" since 1992; and he has distinguished himself in ministry, law and civic leadership. KFIT Radio Station in Austin selected him as the "1998 Pastor of the Year." He has been inducted onto the Board of Preachers of the Martin Luther King, Jr. International Chapel at Morehouse College and serves as president of the Texas Congregations United for Empowerment, Inc. (TCUE).

He is also a Texas attorney and mediator, formerly practicing law as a civil litigator. He has served as the first African American president of the Travis County (Texas) Bar Association, being named as a Trailblazer by the State Bar of Texas, and selected as the Chair of the Board of Advisors of Baylor University's George W. Truett Theological Seminary. He has taught preaching at the George W. Truett Theological Seminary and has taught Advanced Civil Litigation in the Trial Advocacy Program of the University of Texas School of Law. He has utilized his training and background in public administration, law, theology, and urban ministry to inform his ministry and community involvement. He is a graduate of Morehouse College, University of Georgia, Baylor University's George W. Truett Theological Seminary, University of Texas School of Law, and Gordon-Conwell Theological Seminary.

ISBN 1425135714